CHABOT
COLLEGE
LIBRARY

25555 Hesperian Boulevard
Hayward, California 94545

PRINTED IN U.S.A.

REASON IN THEORY AND PRACTICE

Philosophy

_____

Editor

PROFESSOR S. KÖRNER

jur. Dr., Ph.D., F.B.A.

Professor of Philosophy in the
University of Bristol

REASON IN
THEORY AND PRACTICE

Roy Edgley
Senior Lecturer in Philosophy
in the University of Bristol

HUTCHINSON UNIVERSITY LIBRARY
LONDON

HUTCHINSON & CO (*Publishers*) LTD
178–202 Great Portland Street, London W1

London Melbourne Sydney
Auckland Bombay Toronto
Johannesburg New York

First published 1969

*This book has been set in Times, printed in Great Britain
on Smooth Wove paper by Anchor Press, and
bound by Wm. Brendon, both of Tiptree, Essex*

09 098791 8 (paper)
09 098790 X (cased)

TO LIZ
AND CONNIE

CONTENTS

Contents

PREFACE

It is to Eric Gilman, who taught me when I was an undergraduate, that I owe my original interest in the philosophical problems of practical reason. Like most English-speaking philosophers writing on practical reason I am also indebted, though less personally, to R. M. Hare: in the revival of the topic since the last war he has been a major figure, especially, in the fundamental aspects relevant here, through his first book *The Language of Morals*; and the extent of my criticisms of his views is a measure of the importance and influence I attribute to them. But my chief philosophical debt is to D. G. Brown. His conversation and writing, published and unpublished, have decisively and pervasively shaped my ideas on practical reason in particular and reason in general.

Bristol   ROY EDGLEY
January 1969

INTRODUCTION

My aim is to identify some of the most important similarities and differences between theoretical reason and practical reason. What is meant by 'theoretical reason' and what by 'practical reason'? That is a large part of the problem. These are technical terms, and the kinds of things each can be used to cover are not homogeneous. One of my purposes will be to show that common assumptions about the answer to this question can confuse rather than clarify the issues. However, at the moment it is enough to indicate my field of interest in the following way, which will be familiar to those in touch with contemporary discussions. Sometimes, in thinking, we are trying to solve a practical problem, a problem of what to do, a problem that we can symbolise as a question of this general form that we ask ourselves: 'What is to be done?' Sometimes, on the other hand, our thinking is directed to the solution of a theoretical problem, a problem that we can symbolise as a question of this general form that we ask ourselves: 'What is the case?' There has been a lot of philosophical argument about the extent to which problems of these two kinds are capable of a rational solution, about the respective roles of reason in answering questions of these two sorts. This is what my argument is about.

A persistent philosophical claim, especially by empiricists, has been that only theoretical problems are capable of a rational solution and that the role of reason in practical matters, e.g. in morals, is limited by the fact that though practical problems may involve, they are never completely reducible to, theoretical problems. I shall use this doctrine as a starting point for my enquiries and try to distinguish the insights in it to be preserved from the misconceptions to be rejected. The doctrine has, of course, been rejected before, but the dialectical history of the argument shows that in rejecting it we expose ourselves to opposing temptations that equally ought to be resisted. Intuitionism (or ethical rationalism) invites us to treat practical problems as a species of theoretical problems, while other kinds of empiricism, such as some kinds of pragmatism, contend that on the contrary theoretical problems are a species of practical problems. These positions, I suggest, result from largely undiscussed assumptions about the nature of reason as such. I shall try to sketch a more adequate general account of the nature of reason, or at least of some of its relevant aspects.

It is possible to suppose, perhaps under the influence of ideas about philosophical method, that the topic of reason is best approached obliquely. In the entry under *Reason* in *The Encyclopedia of Philosophy* edited by Paul Edwards,[1] G. J. Warnock writes:

. . . whatever particular definition of the faculty of reason we may, implicitly or explicitly, adopt, it seems unavoidable that it will be attempted thereby to distinguish this faculty from others as being that by the exercise of which we can perceive, or arrive at, truths of some particular kind or kinds . . . If so, then the question of what we can actually achieve or come to know by reason unavoidably becomes the question of what propositions are of that kind or those kinds . . . It may further be felt, with justice, that if this innocent-looking question unavoidably raises major philosophical issues concerning the logical and epistemological analysis and classification of propositions, it would probably be advantageous to raise those questions directly or overtly rather than as an only half-acknowledged corollary of a discussion that is ostensibly concerned with a faculty of the mind. There are few modern philosophers who would naturally cast their discussions in this latter idiom.

If this last statement were true, and it is less true now than it was, that would be no cause for congratulation. It may be the case that the special method of philosophy is the analysis of propositions and concepts; on the other hand, if the question is the question of the nature and scope of reason, it would probably be advan-

[1] Macmillan, 1967; quoted by courtesy of Dr Warnock.

tageous, since many propositions explicitly contain that concept, or cognate concepts, to raise that question directly or overtly rather than as an only half-acknowledged corollary of a discussion that is ostensibly concerned with the analysis of propositions not containing those concepts. So far as Warnock is suggesting a one-way traffic between these topics he is advocating an approach that has been seriously misleading, not only about the nature of reason but also about the analysis and classification of propositions in general. One of its most misleading effects can be seen in the second sentence quoted above, where the alleged identity of the two questions and the apposition suggested by 'achieve or come to know by reason' involve a 'cognitive' or theoretical idea of reason that, as I shall show, grotesquely over-simplifies the matter.

A further point about method is perhaps worth making at the outset. In the imprecise terms of philosophical 'subjects', one of my chief areas of interest is the overlap between philosophy of logic and philosophy of psychology or mind. By comparison with the concepts of formal logic, the concepts of psychology are inevitably vague: the concepts we use in talking and thinking about people, ourselves and others, have fairly ill-defined border-lines, so that the drawing of distinctions is a more than usually hazardous business. In these circumstances, however, it is still possible to distinguish and consider the relations of central cases of such concepts. In general, this is what I shall be doing, though I shall also from time to time, where necessary, draw attention to the borderline regions.

I

LOGICAL RELATIONS AND THE THEORETICAL AND LINGUISTIC CONCEPTIONS OF REASON

1.1. *Logic and propositions: the theoretical conception of reason*

What is reason, and why has it been thought to be essentially theoretical and not practical? The words 'reason', 'reasonable', 'unreasonable', 'rational', and 'irrational' are closely connected with the words 'logic', 'logical', and 'illogical', and it is no accident that views about the scope and nature of reason tend to go hand in hand with views about the scope and nature of logic. These words and their cognates cover a wide variety of different items, but it seems likely that these items are connected by a common root; and a simple but plausible way of locating this common root is as follows. Reason, or reasoning, is most typically exercised in arguments or inferences, and an argument is a series of propositions, i.e. truths or falsehoods, in which one proposition is a conclusion or inference from the others, the premises of the argument. If an argument establishes its conclusion the premises are reasons for the conclusion, in other words reasons supporting or proving or justifying the conclusion.

Under scrutiny, this common and unanalysed notion of reason and reasoning reveals itself as capable of distinction and refinement. Two conditions are distinguishable as necessary for an argument to establish its conclusion: the premises must be true; and the inference must be valid, that is, the conclusion must follow from or be in some sense entailed or implied by the premises. These two conditions may be, though they are not necessarily, of fundamentally different natures. In some typical cases the truth of the premises will be an empirical matter, to be settled by perception, observation, or experience, not itself a matter of reason. It is only the other condition that is necessarily a matter for reason itself: the validity or otherwise of the inference, the question of whether the conclusion, true or false, follows from or is entailed or implied by the premises, is not an empirical question but a question of logic, of pure reason, i.e. of reason independently of experience.

Given this distinction, the argument paradigm can be seen as a special case. For the relation of following from, entailment, or implication, which holds between the premises and conclusion of a valid argument, is only one of a family of logical relations, other members of which include such relations as consistency, contradiction, incompatibility, presupposition, and so on. These relations hold between propositions whether or not these propositions occur in arguments or inferences. They may, in fact, be explained in terms of truth and falsehood:

> If x and y cannot both be true,
> then x is inconsistent with y
> and x implies or entails *not-y*.

It is this family of logical relations, it might be said, that provides reason with its general field of operation, and arguments or inferences are only a special, if important, part of that field. What reason essentially does is to discern truths about logical relations. When these relations hold in virtue of the formal characteristics of the propositions involved, these truths of reason are truths of formal logic, and the discipline of formal logic is the systematic identification of such truths of reason.

This idea of reason is the idea of reason as essentially theoretical; for on this view, only propositions, only truths or falsehoods, paradigms of what is theoretical, can have logical relations and be conclusions of arguments or inferences. It is presumably to this idea of reason that Hume commits himself in the *Treatise of Human Nature*, Book III, Part I, Section I, 'Moral distinctions not deriv'd from reason':[1] 'Reason is the discovery of truth and falsehood'. This conception of reason is of course wide enough to be compatible with the possibility of inductive as well as deductive inference: with the possibility, that is, of non-deductive arguments in which empirical conclusions follow from premises that do not

[1] p. 458 of the Selby-Bigge edition.

deductively imply them. This distinction can be briefly explained as follows. If an argument, '*p*, so *q*', is valid, the hypothetical statement in which the premise is the antecedent and the conclusion the consequent, namely 'If *p* then *q*', must be true. If the argument is a valid deductive argument, this hypothetical will be analytic, that is, true solely in virtue of its meaning; whereas if the argument is a valid inductive argument, this hypothetical will be non-analytically true. But whether it is deductive or inductive, both premise and conclusion will be propositions, answers to the theoretical question 'What is the case?'; and the theoretical idea of reason is therefore compatible with the possibility of induction as well as deduction.

What Hume and others have taken the theoretical conception of reason to rule out is the possibility of practical reason. But it does not follow that reason cannot be practical unless it can be shown that practical and theoretical matters are mutually exclusive; and the distinction as I have so far drawn it does not show this. The distinction has been introduced simply in terms of two sorts of questions, 'What is to be done?' and 'What is the case?', and (as an intuitionist might claim) nothing has yet been said to show why the practical question should not be regarded as a species of the theoretical question. For the question 'What is the case?' is the question answered by any answer of the form 'It is the case that . . .', and answers to the practical question can obviously take this form: 'It is the case that so-and-so is to (ought to, should, must) be done'. In other words, answers to practical questions are or can be practical judgments, which are propositions of the sort usually classified by philosophers as value-judgments. As such, they are as much in place as conclusions of inferences or arguments as are propositions of any other kind.

There is a familiar objection to this move, namely that practical answers and judgments are not, properly speaking, answers to the theoretical question 'What is the case?' because, like value-judgments in general, they are not propositions, they cannot be true or false. Now this objection runs counter to the many appearances from which intuitionism draws much of its strength. The normal grammatical form of a practical judgment is a proper indicative sentence, e.g. 'You ought to telephone for the doctor'; and people can ordinarily be said to assert, deny, believe, doubt, be convinced, conclude, infer, or argue, that, e.g., you ought to telephone for the doctor. In these respects, the common conceptual context of practical judgments is the same as that of theoretical judgments, and any adequate account of practical reason must recognise and explain these similarities. Nevertheless, the objection must be allowed this degree of force, that attempts to draw the distinction between theoretical and practical judgments do seem to commit us to the view that the latter contain, as part of their meaning or logic, constituents that debar them from being true or false. For though theoretical as well as practical questions and answers can be about practice, about action, choice, decision, and intention, answers to practical questions seem to be related in such a way to action, choice, decision, and intention, either through emotions, feelings, and attitudes (Hume, and the emotive theories of A. J. Ayer and C. L. Stevenson) or through imperatives (R. M. Hare's prescriptivism), that since these related and relating items cannot be true or false, practical judgments cannot be true or false either. It is this that makes practical judgments evaluative, prescriptive, or normative, rather than descriptive, as empirical judgments are, or analytic.

1.2. *Logic and non-propositions*

The bearing of this question whether practical judgments can be true or false on the question whether reason can be practical has been altered and apparently diminished in various ways in recent years, but specifically by Hare's attack, in *The Language of Morals*,[1] on what can be regarded as this theoretical conception of reason. Hare argues that other things besides propositions can have logical relations. Logical relations are not essentially truth-value relations, i.e. relations of truth and falsehood. Even imperatives, which are incontestably incapable of being true or false, can be consistent or contradictory (as 'Shut the door' is the contradictory of 'Do not shut the door'),[2] and they can therefore stand as premises and conclusions in arguments and inferences. On this view, even though there can be truths of reason, i.e. true statements about the logical relations holding between two or more terms, the terms of those relations are not necessarily truths or falsehoods, and nor, therefore, are conclusions of arguments. Contrary to Hume's claim, reason is not essentially the discovery of truth and falsehood. In particular, though according to Hare practical judgments entail imperatives, this does not debar them from

[1] Oxford, 1952.
[2] op. cit., p. 23.

implying and being implied by other items; and they can, there-fore, be conclusions drawn from premises in an inference.

But from what premises can practical conclusions be validly inferred? A fairly strong idea of practical reason would be that practical judgments can be validly inferred from empirical and in general descriptive premises. But Hare's idea of practical reason is weaker than that. He contends that except when the practical judgments are hypothetical imperatives (judgments of the sort 'If you want to kill the greenfly, spray with insecticide'), they cannot be validly inferred from premises that do not themselves contain a practical judgment: no categorical practical conclusions follow from purely theoretical premises.

In a famous passage in the *Treatise*, Hume observes that the words 'ought' and 'ought not' express a 'relation or affirmation' that is different from that expressed by 'is' and 'is not'; and 'what seems altogether inconceivable', he says, is 'how this new relation can be a deduction from others, which are entirely different from it'.[1] Contrary to some recent suggestions, Hare is right, I think, in reading this as denying, as he himself does, the possibility of validly inferring practical judgments from descriptive premises. For this denial follows from Hume's general idea of reason and his way of drawing the practical-theoretical distinction: what follows is that practical judgments cannot be validly inferred from any premises, descriptive or otherwise. Now Hare repudiates this general idea of reason and so deprives himself of the argument available to Hume in denying the possibility of inference from descriptive to practical judgments. On what grounds, then, can his denial be justified?

One of Hare's chief arguments against this fairly strong con-ception of practical reason[2] appeals to a familiar idea that is central to our interests because it seems to constitute or depend on a theory about the nature and scope of reason itself. It is the idea that rules of inference are analytic and therefore verbal, not substantive, so that the meaning of the conclusion of a valid argument must be contained in the meaning of the premises: all valid inferences, and in general all logical relations, are analytic or deductive. This argument is therefore (as Hare himself sees) restrictive enough to rule out not only the fairly strong idea of practical reason but also inductive reason. Thus Hare's view

[1] op. cit., p. 469.
[2] op. cit., pp. 44–55.

about the scope of reason, though more liberal than the theoretical conception in the range of items it allows as the terms of logical relations, is less liberal in the range of relations it allows. Of course, many philosophers have held both doctrines about reason, and some have held one because of the other; but the considerations Hare brings forward make the distinction clear enough.

1.3. *Logic and action*

To the extent that Hume's scepticism about practical reason, whether the stronger or weaker version of it, depends on his claim that reason is the discovery of truth and falsehood, Hare's demonstration that logical relations are not essentially truth-value relations casts doubt on that scepticism. But there is a different thread of Hume's argument that escapes this objection and which poses a dilemma for the half-way position Hare takes up, his acceptance of the weaker idea of practical reason.

Let us then for the moment ignore the claim that practical judgments are related to action and emotion in such a way that since actions and emotions cannot be true or false, practical judgments, despite appearances, cannot be true or false either. Whether or not only truths and falsehoods can be conclusions of arguments, Hume's scepticism can still rest on this consideration: practical judgments are related to action and emotion in such a way that since actions and emotions cannot be conclusions of arguments or inferences, practical judgments, despite appearances, cannot be conclusions of arguments or inferences either.

In other words, the key items that Hume contrasts with truths and falsehoods, or what he calls judgments and what I have been calling propositions, are actions and emotions. What Hare, on the other hand, contrasts with truths and falsehoods, indicative utterances, are other utterances that cannot be true or false, such as imperatives. The question that Hume in effect poses is this: even if other utterances that are not true or false fall within the purview of reason, do actions and emotions? Can not only statements and imperatives, but also actions and emotions, have logical relations and be conclusions of arguments and inferences? According to Hare, the imperative 'Shut the door' can have logical relations and be a conclusion drawn from premises. The question is, can the action of shutting the door have logical relations and be a conclusion drawn, if not from premises that are true or false empirical statements, at least from premises that are or imply imperatives?

Some such question is surely justified. Hume has got his priorities right in insisting that questions about the rationality of practical judgments, or more generally practical utterances, including moral judgments and imperatives, must be settled by considering the relation of reason to action. At the centre of the concept of the practical in the idea of practical reason is the concept of practice, of action, not the concept of practical utterances or judgments, judgments of action. Neglect of this is one of the chief defects of intuitionism.

1.4. *Logic and meaning: the linguistic conception of reason*

It will be useful to list the items now up for discussion as involved in the practical-theoretical distinction and as falling inside or outside the scope of reason:

(1) Things one can say, or tell somebody, that are incontestably true or false, e.g. that he shut the door, or 'You shut the door'.

(2) Things one can say, or tell somebody, that are contestably true or false, e.g. that he should shut the door, or 'You should shut the door'.

(3) Things one can say, or tell somebody, that are incontestably not true or false, e.g. to shut the door, or 'Shut the door'.

(4) Things one can feel, emotions, passions, or feelings, or attitudes one can take up, such as approval of, anger about, or being in favour of, e.g. your shutting the door.

(5) Things one can do, actions such as shutting the door, and deciding, choosing, or intending to do such things.

Hume aligns his distinction between what can be true or false and what cannot with a distinction between things that are 'representative' and 'original existences'.[1] Items of Group (1), we could say, represent or misrepresent the facts, and in this consists their truth or falsity. But as Hare and others have pointed out, items of Groups (2) and (3) also contain a representing or descriptive element, what Hare calls the phrastic, an element that can be formulated in a noun-phrase designating what the utterance is about, in this example 'Your shutting the door'. Indeed, according

[1] op. cit., p. 415.

to Hare it is possession of a phrastic that enables items of Groups (1), (2), and (3) to have logical relations and so qualifies them as possible conclusions of arguments or inferences. Once it is recognised that logical relations between true or false statements hold in virtue of the meanings of those statements, it can be seen that the province of logic or reason extends to all meaningful utterances, including utterances that are not true or false, such as imperatives, or are only doubtfully so, such as value-judgments. Thus the idea that logical principles, rules of inference, truths of logic or reason, are analytic and verbal seems to imply that logical relations hold only between items of the first three groups, things that can be said or told. This view about the scope of reason I shall call the linguistic conception of reason.

May we then extend the list, to include phrastics themselves, and more generally still, perhaps, simply words? Some logicians and philosophers talk of logical relations between predicates, or concepts, or class-expressions, the relations in this context sometimes being specified as those of inclusion, exclusion, and overlap, though these are systematically related to, e.g. entailment.[1] Hume himself could be regarded as allowing something of this kind. He holds that deductive, or what he calls 'demonstrative', reason 'regards the abstract relations of our ideas',[2] an idea being identifiable, presumably, as the idea of, e.g., his shutting the door, or being a philosopher.

Whether or not the list is in this respect exhaustive, it may also be doubted whether its items are exclusive. Among the things one can say are such things as 'Would that I were in Grantchester' or 'I will shut the door'. As well as falling into one of the first three groups these are clearly closely related to items in Groups (4) and (5). For though items in these groups do not have meanings as words do, we use words both to express our feelings and to announce our decisions and intentions: items in Groups (4) and (5) can be 'put into words'. So also (to take in Hume's point, above) can ideas. Can we then include in the scope of reason not only things that can be said but also things that, though not meaningful in the way that words are, can be put into words?

I shall return to these two possibilities. For the moment, it is enough to observe that neither possibility includes actions. In

---

[1] See, for example, S. Körner, *Conceptual Thinking*, Dover Publications, p. 34.
[2] op. cit., p. 413.

particular, though your shutting the door is something that can be talked about, it is not something that can itself be said, told, or put into words. Hume classifies actions as 'original existences' or 'realities', to be distinguished from ideas, and therefore incapable of having logical relations and being conclusions of arguments. These characteristics, he thinks, actions share with other items in Groups (4) and (5). In these two groups, we may say, we have a collection of things that we can classify crudely as actions and states ascribable to people. Hume called them 'original existences' presumably because like actions and states ascribable to inanimate things, such as the action of the wind on the sand, or the state of the weather, they are or involve, at least in part, a kind of event or occurrence, having chronological and causal relations with natural actions and states but no logical relations with anything. Only descriptions and misdescriptions of such things, and ideas about them, not the things themselves, can have logical relations.

1.5. *A dilemma for the linguistic conception*

Hume's conviction that what can be deduced or inferred must not be 'entirely different' from what it is deduced or inferred from has been common among philosophers.[1] In modern jargon, we could say that what seems inconceivable is that items of different logical types or categories should enter into logical relations allowing an item of one type to be a deduction or inference from an item of another type. In these terms, Hare's view is that imperatives can be inferred from other imperatives, and from value-judgments, because these are of the same logical type, namely prescriptive utterances; but imperatives and value-judgments cannot (with the exception mentioned) be inferred from empirical statements alone, because empirical statements are not prescriptive utterances. We must, I think, accept the claims that imperatives and practical judgments can have logical relations, so that a practical judgment such as 'You ought to shut this door' can be drawn as a conclusion from a practical premise such as 'You ought to shut all these doors'. But there is a dilemma for Hare's half-way position. If practical judgments and empirical statements, which are similar at least in being utterances, are different enough for it to be inconceivable that the former should be inferences from the latter, is it not (even more?) inconceivable that actions, which are not

[1] A contemporary expression of this conviction occurs in D. P. Gauthier's *Practical Reasoning*, p. 17.

utterances at all, and which therefore seem to be of an entirely different category, should stand in this logical relation to utterances of any kind, whether empirical or practical? If they can and do stand in this relation, the linguistic conception of reason, the doctrine that since logical principles are analytic, not substantive, logical relations hold only between utterances, will have to be rejected. If actions cannot stand in any such relation to practical judgments and imperatives, can the claim that such utterances fall within the scope of reason and logic have any bearing on the question whether actions fall within the scope of reason and logic?

What, then, is the relation between the practical judgment that one ought to shut the door, or the imperative 'Shut the door', and the action of shutting the door? Intuitionism, impressed by the appearance of practical judgments as judgments, i.e. as propositions, items that can be true or false, believed, disbelieved, asserted and denied, implies that the relationship is purely contingent. In *Reason and Goodness*,[1] Brand Blanshard, defending intuitionism, or what he calls rationalism, against Hume, says: 'It is perfectly possible to say that my recognition of an act as the right one is a purely intellectual affair, but that I shall not go on to do it unless moved by something else, such as a feeling, desire, or resolution . . . The judgment that one's past keeping of a promise was right . . . is plainly not connected with any election on my part to do the act approved. Here the insight and performance are sharply disconnected'. Hume, like Stevenson after him, seems to think of the relationship as causal: 'Morals excite passions, and produce or prevent actions'.[2] In more recent jargon, practical judgments are practical in the sense that they influence conduct. But is this a causal statement? As has been pointed out,[3] empirical factual statements can have this relationship to action; and indeed, the appearance of the doctrine as an empirical causal one is modified by its tendency to take to itself such forms as 'The essential function of moral judgments is to influence conduct' or 'It is part of the meaning of moral judgments that they express feelings and emotions'. The suggestion here is that the relationship is not causal but logical, and what Hare does is to give an account of it in logical terms.

[1] Allen and Unwin, 1961, pp. 82–3.
[2] op. cit., p. 457.
[3] e.g., by A. MacIntyre in *A Short History of Ethics*, p. 172.

At one point, he seems to allow that actions can be logically derived or deduced from moral judgments, and he tries to reconcile this with the linguistic conception of reason:

The fact that the derivation of particular acts (or commands to do them) from principles is normally done non-verbally does not show that it is not a logical process, any more than the inference

> The clock has just struck seven times
> The clock strikes seven times at seven o'clock only
> ∴ It is just after seven o'clock

is shown to be non-logical because it is never made explicitly in words.[1]

The question that must be asked of this is: does the parenthesis offer a genuine alternative, or is it to be read as a correction or explication of what has gone before? If the act of shutting the door, as distinct from the command 'Shut the door', can be deduced from anything, it is not that this is normally or even always done non-verbally but that it could not be done verbally; and this is enough to distinguish it radically from the inference about the time, and to contradict the linguistic conception of reason.

Hare's more considered doctrine on this matter is that a value-judgment, say that one ought to shut the door, entails a self-addressed imperative, 'Shut the door', and assenting to the imperative, and therefore to the value-judgment, necessarily involves, when the occasion arises and it is in one's power, shutting the door. 'It is a tautology', says Hare,[2] 'to say that we cannot sincerely assent to a second-person command addressed to ourselves, and *at the same time* not perform it, if now is the occasion for performing it and it is in our (physical and psychological) power to do so'. It might seem that here too Hare is arguing that actions can have logical relations and be inferences, for they can be entailed by and inferred from prescriptive premises; in which case his view would be incompatible with Hume's. Yet this may be an illusion. Hare later[3] points out that on his view, strictly interpreted, 'it becomes analytic to say that everyone always does what he thinks he ought to . . .', and this and the passage above seem then to mean not that actions can be infer-

[1] op. cit., pp. 63-4.
[2] op. cit., p. 20.
[3] op. cit., p. 169.

ences from value-judgments but only that statements about actions can be inferences from statements about value-judgments. The claim that the statement 'He thinks he ought to keep promises' entails the statement 'He keeps his promises' is, of course, entirely in harmony both with Hume's view that statements about actions, but not actions themselves, can have logical relations and be inferred from premises, and with the doctrine that logical relations hold in virtue of the meanings of their terms and thus only between utterances, things that can be said.

1.6. *Inference and action*

The idea that actions cannot have logical relations or be conclusions of arguments, which seemed obvious to Hume and has seemed obvious to many of his successors, has not seemed obvious to other philosophers. On the contrary, Aristotle held,[1] without seeing the need to justify the claim, that there could be practical syllogisms whose conclusions are actions. Kant says:[2] 'Since the deduction of actions from principles requires *reason*, the will is nothing but practical reason'. 'An inference', says Wittgenstein,[3] 'is a transition to an assertion; and so also to the behaviour that corresponds to the assertion. "I draw the consequences" not only in words, but also in action'. A contemporary philosopher, A. J. Kenny, writes:[4] 'In practical reasoning as in theoretical we pass from premises to conclusion . . . the conclusions are actions or plans of action'.

Let us face this question squarely: can actions, and not simply things that can be said about actions, be inferred, drawn as conclusions from premises in arguments? As I shall show, the claim that they can has something of importance in it. But as it stands it must be rejected, as Hume rejected it. It involves the conceptual deformity typical of a philosophically one-sided diet, and typical of a peculiarly philosophical diet: a diet unbalanced by a preponderance of theoretical reasoning. As Hume's supporters could argue, the key notions of implying, following from, inferring, deducing, and drawing conclusions from premises, simply do not fit in the places allotted to them by this version of

---

[1] e.g. the *Nicomachean Ethics*, 1147a 25–32, and the *Movement of Animals*, 701a 7–20.
[2] *Fundamental Principles of the Metaphysic of Morals*, second section.
[3] *Philosophical Investigations*, 486.
[4] 'Practical Inference', *Analysis*, January 1966.

the idea of practical reason. Whatever the logical implications of the judgment 'You ought to shut the door' or the order 'Shut the door', your shutting the door cannot be one of them; it cannot follow, or be inferred or deduced, from these items or from any others, nor can it be drawn as a conclusion from these or any other premises.

Barbarisms that seem to deny this could be given an acceptable interpretation, but not one that would support this formulation of the idea of practical reason. For instance, your shutting the door might be said to follow from or be a conclusion or consequence of the judgment in the sense of following after and being an effect of that judgment; but the relation here would be chronological and causal, not logical. Or it might be said that your shutting the door followed from, or could be inferred, deduced, or concluded from, say, the facts; but this could mean only that what was here said to follow, or be inferred, deduced, or concluded from the facts was that you shut the door, or that you should shut the door. It is certainly possible to infer what someone does; but to suppose that this supports the idea of practical reason being considered would be a mistake of the kind pointed out by J. L. Austin in his paper *Other Minds*.[1] The 'what' here is not the relative 'that which' but the interrogative. The statement 'I inferred what he did' does not mean that there is something that both I inferred and he did, but that I inferred, e.g., that he shut the door, the expression introduced by the word 'that' being an answer to the question 'What did he do?'. Now of course, having inferred what he did, I could answer this question not by putting into words what I had inferred, i.e. by saying 'He shut the door', but by showing what he did by doing it myself, i.e. by shutting the door. Actions cannot be put into words, but what can be put into words can sometimes also be enacted, or shown by action. But in showing what he did, my shutting the door would only show what I inferred, it would not be what I inferred.

'What he did' is only one of a sizable range of interrogative phrases that can follow the word 'infer': others are those that can be introduced by the interrogatives 'who', 'when', 'where', 'why', and 'how'. Austin's argument is about the word 'know', and this word too, like 'infer', can be followed by any of this range of interrogative phrases. It might be thought, then, that Ryle's argument in *The Concept of Mind* would show that *inferring how*

[1] p. 64 of the reprint in *Philosophical Papers*.

is to be distinguished from *inferring that* as *knowing how* is distinguished from *knowing that*, and that this would support the idea of practical reason that I am repudiating; for, it might be said, I could come to know how by inferring how, and what I would here be inferring would be the actions or performances constituting the exercise of my know-how or skill. But this is a muddle. Let us distinguish knowing and inferring how *he* shut the door (say the door of the safe, which is too heavy and has too complicated a lock to shut in the normal way), from knowing and inferring how *to* shut the door. It seems clear that in this kind of case there is no antithesis between knowing or inferring *how* and knowing or inferring *that*, whether the *how* is *how he* or *how to*. Knowing and inferring how are here no more species of knowing and inferring coordinate with knowing and inferring that than are knowing and inferring what, who, when, where, or why. In all these cases, what is known or inferred is the answer to the question formulated by these interrogative phrases: e.g. I know or infer *that* he shut the door by pressing the button and turning the knob, and I know or infer *that* the way to shut the door is to press the button and turn the knob. These questions and answers are, of course, formulated in indirect speech: what is true is that somebody may know something without being able to say what he knows, but this distinction between knowing and being able to say cuts across any distinction that might be drawn between knowing how and knowing that, holding for the latter as well as for the former. In either case, someone who is unable to say what he knows may show what he knows by his actions, as by doing something one may show what one infers. What is also true is that when doing something is itself more or less skilled or sophisticated, as driving a car or riding a bicycle is by comparison with shutting the door of the safe by simply pressing a button and turning a knob, knowing how to do that thing does normally entail being able to do it. But in this continuum, the nearer we get to this kind of case the more appropriate will become the notion of the practice of learning how and the less appropriate the notion of inferring how.

Unlike actions, the other items of Group (5) in my list, and the items of Group (4), can be expressed in or put into words; but even this is not enough to make it possible for them, in contrast to propositions reporting them, to be inferred from anything. Hume was right in thinking that, like actions, passions cannot be conclusions of arguments. A pertinent philosophical joke comes from W. S. Gilbert, whose Patience sings:

> Nobody I care for
> Comes a-courting—therefore
> Hey willow waly O!

Similarly odd would be any attempt to introduce an expression of a wish, or longing, such as 'Would that I were in Grantchester', with the words 'I infer . . .' or 'I infer that . . .'. Even when a that-clause is available, as in the expression of a wish that takes the verbal form of an empirical statement of fact, the oddity remains: 'I infer that I wish that I were in Grantchester'. It is to be noticed that there is no corresponding oddity about the utterance 'So I wish that I were in Grantchester', as it might follow, say, 'She'll be there now'. The form 'p, so q' is not necessarily the form of an inference. This comes out equally clearly with announcements of decisions and intentions: e.g. 'It's cold, so I shall shut the door'. If this is a statement of my intention to shut the door, I can be said to know or think that I shall shut the door, and it might be thought that this belief or piece of knowledge is here non-inductively inferred from the fact that it is cold. But the truth is that it is not inferred at all, inductively or non-inductively. The effect of prefacing my announcement with the words 'I infer that . . .' would be to convert my statement 'I shall shut the door' into a prediction that is not a statement of intention.

1.7. *Imperative inference: a condition*

These considerations support Hume's doctrine that actions and passions cannot be conclusions of arguments. For they all imply that the only sort of thing that can be inferred, deduced, or concluded, is *that* something-or-other is the case, where this is a theoretical judgment in the sense of one that does not essentially express an emotion or a decision or intention to do something. Indeed, if this is true they are incompatible with Hare's weaker thesis that there is such a thing as imperative inference.

It can at least be admitted, I think, that theoretical judgments in the above sense, expressed in complete indicative sentences introduced by the word 'that', are paradigms of what can be inferred or deduced or concluded from premises. Extensions of the notion of inference away from this paradigm should be justified. Now it is true that imperatives can have logical relations. The range of the notion of consistency is wide enough to ensure this: an officer can issue consistent or inconsistent orders. And it might be thought that this is all that is needed to give a use to the concept of inferring imperatives that is close enough to the paradigm to justify it. Rejecting the ideas of truth and falsehood as essential, and taking instead the notion of consistency as basic, we could explain other logical relations in terms of it, and the notion of valid inference in terms of them, as follows:

> If x is inconsistent with y,
> then x implies or entails *not-y*,
> and *not-y* can be validly inferred from x.

But though organising these concepts into this tightly knit network may be harmless enough within the fairly narrow and well-defined limits of a special field of formal logic, this is not enough when the question is about the nature and limits of reason in general. I have so far gone along with what seems to be a fairly widespread practice among philosophers, of talking of logical relations and inference in the same breath. But the fact is that though these concepts are members of the family of reason, that family is an extended family containing different nuclear groups, and these different groups have different relations with other groups and families of concepts. It may be true that if x can be validly inferred from y, then y is inconsistent with *not-x*. It does not follow that if y is inconsistent with *not-x*, then x can be validly inferred from y. I have already mentioned, in the rough and ready account of reason given earlier, that in an argument or inference two different elements can be distinguished: the validity of the inference, and the establishment of the conclusion. An argument establishes its conclusion if the inference is valid and the premises are true. Now it might be thought that though imperatives cannot be true or false or possess any similar characteristic, nevertheless imperative inference is possible because the validity of an inference depends only on the logical relation of implication or entailment between premises and conclusion, and not at all on their truth or falsehood. But this is confused. If we thin out the requirements still further in a way already indicated, and allow logical relations between simply words and phrases such as phrastics or predicates, it is clear that the concept of inference cannot survive unaided in this rarefied atmosphere. If we allow, for example, that 'green' entails 'coloured',[1] we must abandon the above schema: it is unintelligible to claim that 'coloured' can be validly inferred from 'green', where this is not equivalent to the claim that from the fact that something is green one can infer that it is coloured. Though the question of the validity of an inference is different from the question whether what is validly inferred is also established, it is not independent of the question whether what is said to be validly inferred is the sort of thing that can be established. Valid inference is possible only where inference is possible; inference is possible only where one can say not merely 'From x one can (or could, if x were true) infer y' but also 'From x I infer y'; and to say this is not simply to say that x and *not-y* are inconsistent, it is to accept or commit oneself to y in the way that one commits oneself to what one accepts or asserts (i.e. believes) to be true. Hare's view is that assenting to an imperative, i.e. acting or being prepared to act on it, is analogous to accepting a statement of fact.[2] But a statement can be true or false, and the idea of accepting a statement is logically tied to the idea of possibly accepting a false statement, and so of being mistaken in a way that is independent of that statement's inconsistency with the other statements one accepts. If there is no analogue of this with imperatives, i.e. if assenting to an imperative cannot be mistaken in a way that is independent of that imperative's inconsistency with the other imperatives one assents to, the fact that imperatives have logical relations will not show that there can be such a thing as imperative inference.

1.8. *Hume: reason's role in action*

Though denying that actions can be inferred from anything, Hume did, of course, admit that we can think about what to do, that some of this thinking can be reasoning, and that this reasoning can have an effect on our conduct; and these admissions lead him to put his doctrine about practical reason in the words 'reason alone can never produce any action'.[3] The implication of the word 'alone' is that conduct can be influenced by reason together with something else, namely a passion, emotion, or feeling of some sort. And this may seem incompatible with his arguments on

[1] An example from Körner, op. cit., p. 15.
[2] op. cit., pp. 18–20.
[3] op. cit., p. 414.

reason as I have so far described them, arguments that Hume himself claims prove that 'reason is perfectly inert' and that 'Reason is wholly inactive'.[1] If reason is perfectly inert, how can it even help to influence our actions and emotions? The answer is summed up as follows: 'a passion must be accompany'd with some false judgment, in order to its being unreasonable; and even then 'tis not the passion, properly speaking, which is unreasonable, but the judgment'.[2] It is clear that in Hume's view this doctrine about passions applies equally to actions.

To illustrate his point: I see a dog, which I think is dangerous, and so I feel afraid and run away. My action of running away and my emotion of fear can be reasonable or unreasonable only so far as they are accompanied with the judgment that the dog is dangerous. This judgment can be true or false and therefore a conclusion of reason, something that can be inferred from other such items constituting the premises of a possible argument. But my fear and my running away are not of this sort: they cannot be conclusions of arguments, or follow from premises. Their relation to the judgment is that of being 'accompanied with' it. I could correctly report the situation in the words 'The dog was dangerous *and* I felt afraid and ran away'; or more strongly, 'The dog was dangerous *and so* I felt afraid and ran away' or 'I felt afraid and ran away *because* the dog was dangerous'. Hume's idea would be that the conjunction 'and' and the connectives 'and so' and 'because' express not the logical relation of a conclusion to its premises but at most a psychological causal relation between the judgment on the one hand, and the feeling and action on the other.

It might be objected to this that as far as I am concerned these would be causes 'known without observation', to use G. E. M. Anscombe's phrase.[3] But this would be an objection to Hume's account of causality, not to his account of the relation of reason to action and passion. Or it might be objected that the relation between thinking something dangerous and feeling afraid of it cannot be simply causal, even if we allow some causes to be known without observation; for a feeling could not properly be called one of fear unless the object of the feeling was something thought to be dangerous. On this view thinking that something is dangerous is an analytically necessary condition of being afraid

[1] op. cit., p. 458.
[2] op. cit., p. 416.
[3] *Intention*, § 9.

of it. But though this seems to be true, what it means is that 'I am afraid of it' and 'He is afraid of it' respectively imply 'I think it's dangerous' and 'He thinks it's dangerous'. It does not mean that 'He's afraid of it' follows from 'He thinks it's dangerous', or that feeling afraid can be inferred from the judgment that it's dangerous. Feeling afraid of something is not identical with judging it to be dangerous, and whatever else there is in fear, what makes us classify it as a feeling or emotion, distinguishing it from a thought or judgment, is something whose relation to that or any other judgment can only, on the view we are considering, be psychological and causal, not the logical relation of conclusion to premise. Thus if you persuaded me that the dog was not dangerous, my feeling towards it could no longer be described as 'fear'; but I could still dislike or feel averse to it in some other way, and what I actually felt and did, if anything, would depend, like my original fear, on my beliefs and other feelings at the time, this dependence again being causal and not logical. Thus neither the claim that 'feeling afraid of it' entails 'thinking it dangerous', nor the analogous claim that evaluative language is partly descriptive, constitutes an objection to Hume's thesis. That thesis could be summarised as follows: actions and emotions cannot be conclusions of reason and cannot therefore be effects of reason alone; but they can be effects of reason in conjunction with other emotions.

1.9. *Reason and reality, liberalism and romanticism*

Common to both Hume's theoretical conception of reason and the more modern linguistic conception of reason is the assumption that the range of items that fall within the scope of reason is identical with the range of items that can be inferred. Purged of both its Platonistic possibilities and the psychological tendencies in Hume's language and thought, his doctrine that inference is possible in virtue of relations between ideas has survived in modern empiricism as the doctrine that rules of inference are analytic or verbal, logical relations holding only between things that can be said. Both in this and Hume's version, a gap is opened up between reason and reality, between what is inert and non-substantive and the substantive and active reality of facts, actions, and passions. Allegiance to reason understood in this way has been partly responsible for the spread of liberal views about toleration and non-violence, a belief in reason being identified with a belief in reasoning, inferring, or arguing, and a preference for thoughts and words rather than deeds and feelings. The Romantic rejection of reason in favour of the 'subjective' reality of personal emotion and action was and is to some extent a rejection of reason understood in this way. My aim is to show that what really needs rejecting is not reason, but this conception, or rather misconception, of it.

2

PSYCHOLOGICAL VERBS AND THE
PRACTICAL CONCEPTION OF REASON

2.1. *Logical and psychological verbs*

I have already said, and said something to support the contention, that despite their common membership of the family of concepts of reason, concepts signifying logical relations form a different nuclear group from those of inference, deduction, argument, and conclusion. The distinction is obscured, harmlessly enough for formal logic, by the logician's device of representing inferences, arguments, and conclusions as propositions set out in familiar written or printed patterns, so that one proposition can be said to be an inference or conclusion from another as well as an implication of it. But these nouns have verbal forms which, unlike the verbal forms of logical relation nouns, seem to designate not abstract relations but things that people do, and in particular things that only people, not propositions, can do. Propositions and theories can imply, entail, and follow from other things of a similar sort. But only people (or more cautiously, only rational beings) can argue, deduce, infer, and conclude, that is, draw conclusions; and in general, it is people who think and reason. Moreover, when it is true that somebody argues, deduces, infers, or concludes that something is the case, this is true as a matter of empirical fact, not as a matter of logic or reason: it is true of the person concerned, and in particular tells us something about his mind. In other words, these are psychological verbs, in contrast to the verbs designating logical relations, such as 'implies', 'entails', 'contradicts', etc., which we could call 'logical' verbs.

This is a distinction between these concepts, not a disconnection. Indeed, even the distinction can seem to break down when we observe that 'implies' and 'contradicts', for instance, can take personal subjects, and 'contradicts' a personal object, and can be used as the main verbs in contingent statements of fact rather than necessary truths of logic, as in 'Smith contradicted Jones and implied that Robinson would be late'. However, it could be argued that this psychological use of these verbs implies their logical use, and not vice versa. Smith could contradict Jones and imply that Robinson would be late only by saying something, and only if what he said, that is, in the jargon, only if the proposition he uttered, contradicted what Jones said and implied that Robinson would be late; whereas what Smith said could have these logical relations without its being true that the implying and contradicting could be properly attributed to Smith, since he might be unaware of these relations. As I have suggested, 'implies' and 'contradicts', but not 'infers', can fill the gap in 'The proposition that p . . . the proposition that q'. The nearest one can get to this construction with 'infers' and its cognates is 'The proposition that p is an inference from the proposition that q', and a statement of this sort, unlike the one with 'implies', means the same as one of a different construction not available with 'implies', namely 'The proposition that p can be inferred from the proposition that q'. What this, unlike a statement of implication, seems to presuppose is that someone may not infer something that he could infer, as someone may not shut the door though he could shut it.

An important connection between these two groups of concepts is that the sorts of things that can be inferred, and the sorts of things they can be inferred from, are the sorts of things that can have logical relations. I have already argued that in inferring one thing from another one accepts what one infers in the way in which one accepts a proposition, as something asserted, thought, or believed to be true. Here too, then, related to the terms of logical relations as inference is, we have another set of concepts designated by verbs that take personal subjects and which seem, like 'argue', 'infer', 'deduce', and 'conclude', to be verbs of action or activity. Answering to the view that logical relations hold between linguistic entities there are some of the verbs studied by Austin in *How To Do Things With Words*, verbs denoting speech acts and things done in and by performing speech acts (locutionary, illocutionary, and perlocutionary acts): among the central members for our purposes are 'say', 'tell', 'assert', and 'deny'.

Answering to the view that logical relations hold between psychological entities such as ideas there are some members of the group of psychological verbs: these include 'think', 'believe', 'disbelieve', 'know', 'judge', 'accept', and 'reject'.

2.2. *The practical conception of reason*

The occurrence of these concepts in key positions in the general notion of reason may make it seem that our original distinction between practical and theoretical as coordinate species of questions and answers, and of the thinking that issues in those answers, was misconceived, as intuitionism contends, but in the opposite way to the way intuitionism suggests. It is not, it seems, that the practical is a species of the theoretical, but on the contrary that the theoretical is a species of the practical. Answering the theoretical question 'What is the case?' is saying, asserting, or believing something, and as these are kinds of doing this question is indistinguishable from the practical question 'What is to be said, asserted, or believed?', which is a special case of the general practical question 'What is to be done?'. Furthermore, it may be said, the inferring, thinking, and reasoning that issue in the answer are all kinds of doing, linguistic or psychological or both, and rules of logic or inference are thus a kind of principle of conduct licensing these operations of inferring, thinking, and concluding, and ultimately, perhaps, linguistic rules governing the saying of things. I shall call this 'the practical conception of reason'. From what has been said it is clear that like the theoretical conception the practical conception of reason has a linguistic version; but for reasons that I hope will become apparent I shall not treat this separately.

Aspects of this position are to be found in several fairly recent publications. Ryle says in his inaugural lecture *Philosophical Arguments*[1] 'There are . . . many disciplines which teach not truths but arts and skills, such as agriculture, tactics, music, architecture, painting, games, navigation, inference, and scientific method'; and in *The Concept of Mind* (though the position is not consistently maintained), 'we mean by "inference" an operation which the thinker must be able to repeat . . . arguments . . . are . . . like skills . . . we should have thought of the rules of logic rather as licences to make inferences than as licences to concur in them'.[2]

[1] p. 3.
[2] pp. 300–6.

Hare[1] writes: 'Principles of prediction are one kind of principle of action; for to predict is to act in a certain way'; and[2] '. . . what is taught is in most cases a principle. In particular, when we learn *to do* something, what we learn is always a principle. Even to learn or be taught a fact (like the names of the five rivers of the Punjab) is to learn how to answer a question; it is to learn the principle "When asked 'What are the names of the five rivers of the Punjab?' answer 'The Jhelum, the Chenab, etc.' " '. In *The Uses of Argument*, though rejecting 'the idea that inferring is a kind of performance to be executed in accordance with rules',[3] Toulmin nevertheless says of logical criticism:[4] 'it treats an utterance as an action performed in a given situation, and asks about the merits of this action when looked at in the context of its performance'.

I shall try to show in the next chapter what can be salvaged from these ideas. Here and now I shall argue that as philosophical doctrines about what principles of inference and prediction and logical criticism essentially are they are unacceptable. If there is an argument for practical reason these doctrines do not provide it: the matters they draw attention to are compatible with the claim that principles of inference and prediction are not principles of action and that logical epithets are applicable to other items than actions.

2.3. *Saying and what is said*

To start with Hare and Toulmin, it is certainly true that saying or uttering something is a kind of doing, and that predicting is or may be a kind of saying. Principles of conduct could, then, include principles concerning predicting, saying, and uttering things. 'Don't say "Damn" in front of a lady' might be a rule of manners; 'Don't predict in the patient's hearing that he won't get better' might be a rule in the ethical code of a doctor's medical practice. It is another question whether all principles that could be called principles of prediction are principles of conduct, and whether logical criticism, which is commonly distinguished from moral criticism and criticism of manners, is of actions.

Let us suppose that Smith says 'You will be late', and that this prediction contravenes the 'principles of prediction' by laying

[1] op. cit., p. 59.
[2] p. 60.
[3] p. 5.
[4] p. 181.

itself open to the logical criticism that it is inconsistent with the evidence. First of all, Toulmin is right in implying that to know this we need to look at Smith's speech act 'in the context of its performance'. We need to know not only that Smith uttered the words 'You will be late', but that he uttered them yesterday, and was referring to Jones and his meeting tomorrow. We also need to know what illocutionary act Smith was performing, since these words could be used to give an order rather than to make a prediction. But this does not imply that what is inconsistent with the evidence is Smith's speech-act. What is inconsistent with the evidence is not what Smith did but what he said. Even if what somebody does is to say something, knowing and understanding what he does is not to be confused with knowing and understanding what he says. As Wittgenstein's example shows,[1] someone's action in saying something may be intelligible even though what he says is unintelligible nonsense: you may utter a meaningless string of words, and you may mean to do so, your point or purpose being, for example, to shock or surprise somebody. When what somebody says is intelligible, I need, in order to know whether it is, for instance, consistent or inconsistent with the evidence, to understand what he does more fully than is involved in understanding what he says in direct speech; but I need to understand more fully what he does only in order to understand more fully what he says. It is of this that the logical criticism can be made, and this in its relation to the evidence that can conform to or contravene the 'principles of prediction'. To say that the prediction is inconsistent with the evidence is to say that on the evidence it is very likely false, and as Strawson has argued,[2] the notions of truth and falsity apply not to the saying of things but to what is said. Smith's prediction is identified as: that Jones will be late; and it is the prediction in this sense, what is predicted, distinguished from the predicting of it by Smith or anybody else, that can be the target of the logical objection that it is contrary to the evidence.

Given this distinction we can see something of what lies behind the idea that logical and moral criticism, logical and moral principles, are distinct: they are, it might be said, of different sorts of things. A prediction may thus be logically impeccable but

[1] op. cit., 498.
[2] Symposium on 'Truth', *Proceedings of the Aristotelian Society,* supplementary volume XXIV, 1950.

morally objectionable. That the patient will die may be true and supported by the evidence, but predicting this, e.g. in the patient's hearing, may cause unnecessary suffering.

The obvious objection to Hare's point about learning a fact is that if I learn, e.g., that my neighbour's 'long holiday' last year was in fact a period in gaol, I do not thereby learn the principle 'When asked (say by the local gossip) "Where did he go for his holiday last year?" answer "To gaol" '. The most that could be said along these lines would be that what I have learned in learning the fact is how to answer the question truthfully; and all this seems to mean is that what I have learned is the true answer to the question, which in itself does not imply that I should answer the question truthfully rather than deceitfully, or even that I should answer it at all. Of course, as Hare points out, our knowledge of factual truths can have a bearing on action through their connection with hypothetical imperatives, but he does not show that the alleged relation between knowing the facts and the action of answering questions is any more than a special case of this general relationship.

It is clear that part of what is involved in correcting in these ways any simple identification of speech acts with items to which logical epithets are applicable, and in the process insisting on the distinction between saying something and what is said, is that what is said may also be left unsaid, kept to oneself, just thought. One's thoughts, in this sense, must be something that can in principle, like one's ideas, feelings, and intentions, be put into words or expressed, but what one thinks is something that need not be and may not be said. There are here two distinctions: first, between on the one hand what is said or thought, and on the other saying or thinking it; and second, between on the one hand saying something and on the other thinking it. Though the distinction between saying something and what is said seems wide enough to provide us with what looks like a fairly clear distinction between moral and logical epithets, the distinction between thinking something and what is thought seems rather less satisfactory for this purpose. Logical epithets apply equally to what is said and what is thought. But whereas what is said may be logically impeccable, though saying it morally objectionable, no such possibility seems open for the distinction between what is thought and thinking it: if what you think is logically acceptable, thinking it cannot be morally objectionable in the way that saying it can.

2.4. *Mental acts: two kinds of thinking*

These considerations suggest a more plausible group of candidates than speech acts for the role of undermining the idea of practical and theoretical matters as coordinate species, and with it Hume's argument against the possibility of practical reason: the 'mental acts' of thinking, believing, accepting, judging, agreeing, etc.; and connected with them, in a way already outlined, inferring, deducing, or concluding. These concepts must occupy a central position in any account of reason. That type of thinking known as reasoning, it could be argued, typically involves acts of inferring, from what we already believe, things that we thus come to believe. The speech act that expresses these steps is the act of saying some such thing as 'So-and-so is the case; *therefore* (or *so*) such-and-such is the case'. On this account of the subject, principles of inference are rules of (mental) conduct, rules licensing the act of inferring one thing from another.

Saying something is certainly doing something, and what is questionable there is not whether this is action but whether it is such actions, rather than what is said or thought, that have logical characteristics. But what is most questionable in this new doctrine is whether thinking and inferring are actions.

The above account mentions two kinds of thinking. There is that kind of thinking known specifically as reasoning or arguing, as when we think or reason or argue something out. In this kind of thinking a question is up for answer, a question that can be introduced in indirect speech into the specification of what the thing is about: e.g., whether there will be a slump. If successful, this kind of thinking issues in thinking of the other kind, namely thinking that so-and-so, where what is thought is something that is an answer to the question considered, e.g., that there will be a slump next year. According to the practical conception of reason, inferring is reaching this conclusion.

There can be no doubt that thinking of the former kind is doing something in a fairly strong sense. Though not an action, it can properly be described as an activity. Like walking, singing, or driving, it can take time and energy, and be easy or difficult, tiring, boring, absorbing, or exhilarating. It is something that one can wonder whether to do and when to do, something one can choose, decide, intend, and try to do. The perfect and continuous tenses of these verbs are typically different in their uses: 'he is thinking about the economic situation', like 'he is walking to the station', 'he is singing in his bath', and 'he is driving to the pub', typically refers to something he is at this moment engaged in; whereas 'he thinks about the economic situation', 'he walks to the station', 'he sings in his bath', and 'he drives to the pub' all typically refer not to something he is at this moment engaged in but to something he does periodically, and could normally be completed by such additions as 'whenever he gets the time' or 'on rainy days' or 'every morning' or 'each Saturday after the game'. The fact that someone is engaged, or periodically engages, in these activities can be explained in terms of his purposes or aims: 'in order to write an article', 'to exercise his mind (legs, lungs)', 'to get there before closing time'.

By these tests, thinking that so-and-so, like believing that so-and-so, is typically not an activity. Suppose I think that there will be a slump next year. Like thinking about whether there will be a slump, my thinking that there will be can begin at a certain moment, go on for a certain length of time, and then stop. But it cannot *take* time, or energy. It may have taken several weeks for it to occur to me, or for me to realise, that there would be a slump; but its occurring to me, or my realising it, is not something that the idea or I spend several weeks doing, as I can spend several weeks thinking about the economic situation. Nor can I typically be said to intend or aim to think that there will be a slump; and connected with this is the fact that however my thinking that there will be a slump is explained, an explanation in terms of my purposes or aims, e.g. 'in order to do something else', or 'with the aim or purpose of doing something else', is at least very abnormal and marks the thinking as so abnormally defective as to rule out any first-person present tense use of this type of explanation.

2.5. *Thinking, believing, and action*

If thinking that so-and-so is not an activity, is it then an action or act? In particular, if this thinking is the outcome of reasoning something out, can it be identified with the act of drawing the conclusion or inferring that so-and-so? In many of its most central cases, thinking that so-and-so is indistinguishable from believing that so-and-so; and in these cases, thinking is not an act or action.[1]

[1] See Alice's encounter with the White Queen in chapter V, 'Wool and Water', of Lewis Carroll's *Through the Looking Glass*.

'Believe' has no continuous tenses, or at least none that is distinguishable in meaning from its perfect tenses. 'He is believing that there will be a slump next year' is an oddity for which there is no special use except perhaps to distinguish an Irish idiom for 'He believes that there will be a slump next year'. For though I may have for several weeks believed that there will be a slump, as I may have for several weeks started my car by pushing it, a statement of this latter kind refers to an action I perform repeatedly, e.g. each morning, so that each morning at a particular moment it could be said of me in the continuous present 'He is starting his car by pushing it'. Nothing of this kind is referred to by the former statement. Of course, for several weeks I may have said repeatedly, to myself or others, that there will be a slump; but not necessarily, and even if I had performed these speech acts each morning it could still have been true of me in the afternoons that I believed that there will be a slump.

There are, it is true, various uses of the concepts of thinking and believing in which they occur in contexts that are typical for action concepts. I can find something easy to believe or difficult to believe, I can be willing or unwilling, ready or reluctant, to believe it, and I can try to believe it or refuse to believe it. 'Believe' has an imperative form in 'Believe me, there'll be a slump next year'.[1] But though these cases warn us against any simple alignment of the practical-theoretical distinction with the categorical gulf between actions and propositions, they do not show that believing is an action. Feeling sorry for somebody is also something one can find easy or difficult, and one can try or refuse to feel sorry for somebody. One cannot intend or decide either to feel sorry or to believe something.

2.6. *Episodic thinking and believing*

Sometimes, thinking that so-and-so is distinguishable from believing that so-and-so; and when it is, the thinking is episodic, and is very closely connected with saying (not aloud but) to oneself that so-and-so (not to be confused with talking to oneself). For instance, a piece of mental biography might run like this: 'He saw

---

[1] In Donne we find:

> Think then, my soul, that death is but a groom,
> Which brings a taper to the outward room . . .
>
> (*The Second Anniversary*)

Is this a 'self-addressed' imperative?

the spots and thought that it was measles'. Alternatives would be: '. . . and thought (said) to himself that it was measles', or '. . . and thought (said) to himself "It's measles"'. In this kind of case one can suddenly think, or thing momentarily, that so-and-so; and continuous tenses are not entirely out of place, as in 'He was just thinking that it was measles when the doctor said "Mumps"'. Given the right circumstances, this kind of thinking can be inferring: 'He saw the spots and inferred that it was measles', or 'He saw the spots and thought (said) to himself "So it's measles"'.

Are these incidents of inferring and thinking that so-and-so actions or acts? That does not follow and is not true. These cases of thinking, more than most others, can typically be redescribed in terms that cast the thinker in a passive rather than an active role: 'When he saw the spots it occurred to him that it was measles'. They resist equally such contexts as 'He intended to think . . .' and 'His purpose in thinking . . .'. And the continuous tense is still an oddity, connecting thinking with saying in that full-fledged sense of saying in which it involves talking to some-body (if only to oneself), but distinguishable from it because 'He was thinking that it was measles' implies 'He thought that it was measles': even though his thoughts when he is thinking that it was measles can be interrupted, they cannot be interrupted as saying can, with the thinking that it was measles only half completed, as saying that it was measles can get as far as 'It's me——' and then be interrupted. As to the verb 'infer', it has no continuous tenses at all, even of this vestigial kind.

These verbs lack normal continuous tenses because, like 'achievement words',[1] they specify something occurring at a moment in time but not occupying a period of time. Driving to the pub may take ten minutes; but the moment of arrival or reaching it is a moment, not a period, long or short. But pubs and the like are not the only things one can reach or arrive at. One can reach or arrive at a position, view, theory, conclusion, or what not, on the question whether, for example, it's measles that he's got. Is it the case, then, that the episodic sense of thinking that it's measles is such an arrival, and that when this arrival is an achievement of reasoning this episode is one of inferring?

If 'It's measles' was a sound inference when he first thought that it was measles, its soundness will not (subject to some qualifica-

[1] Ryle, op. cit., p. 149 ff.

tions that do not alter my point) be affected by the passage of time. He may later recount this episode in his mental history by saying, in the past tense, 'From the fact that he had spots I inferred that it was measles' or 'I saw his spots and realised that it was measles' or 'I saw his spots and thought "So it's measles" '. But if he thinks now that his inference then was sound, he will be able to repeat his words now, but significantly changing the tense of 'inferred' and 'thought' to the present: 'From the fact that he had spots I infer that it was measles', and 'I saw his spots and think that it was measles' or 'He had spots, so it was, I think, measles'. Now these present tense uses of 'infer' and 'think' are clearly not episodic. It is not that having first thought that he had measles when he first saw the spots, he thinks it again, for a second, third, or fourth time, now and whenever he repeats these words. He does not *repeatedly* think that he had measles, as he may repeatedly arrive at the pub, night after night. This is the use of 'think' that is indistinguishable from 'believe'. And in these respects 'infer' follows 'think'.[1] I may say repeatedly 'From the fact that he had spots I infer that it was measles', but I do not repeatedly infer that it was measles. These conceptual points are connected with another: the relation between what one *can* infer and what one infers is radically different from the relation between what one can do and what one does. If I know that I'm in one place, say Bristol, and that one can reach or arrive in London from Bristol by, say, 6 pm, I may then consider whether to arrive in London at that or any other time. But if I know that he's got spots and that one can infer from this fact that he's got measles, there is no further question of whether to infer it. In this respect 'infer' is like verbs of perception: if I can see him walking down the street, then I see him walking down the street.

The episodic uses of 'think that . . .' and 'infer' are parasitic on the non-episodic ones. It would be a mistake to say 'He inferred (thought to himself) that it was measles' unless he could at that moment truly say of himself, in the non-episodic use, 'I infer (think) that it's measles'. In the absence of this condition these episodes are correctly described in some other way, e.g. 'He thought of measles' or 'He had the idea that it might be measles', or 'The possibility of measles suddenly occurred to him'. But this condition is not reversible. A man may, in the non-episodic

[1] As D. G. Brown points out in 'The Nature of Inference', *The Philosophical Review*, July 1955.

present, infer or think that something is the case, without there ever having been a moment at which he inferred or thought to himself that it is the case.

2.7. *Uninterpreted logical calculi as games*

Before I leave this subject I want to mention briefly a legitimate 'practical' interpretation of rules of inference in formal logic, but one which, properly understood, is not incompatible with my arguments. A deductive system, say the truth-functional system of unanalysed propositions, can be represented by an uninterpreted calculus in which the 'symbols' are construed no longer as symbols but as marks on paper to be manipulated as pieces in a game. The advantage of this, of course, is that the correctness of what in the interpreted system would be deductions or inferences is determined in the uninterpreted calculus in a mechanical way, the rules of inference, e.g. 'From p and $p \supset q$ one can infer that q' being interpreted as rules of the game, e.g. 'Given p and $p \supset q$ one may write down q'. In place of 'infer' we have here the action verb 'write down'; and this action verb may itself be interpreted in terms of what a machine, a computer, can do. In this way, what is inessential in determining the correctness of the inference is eliminated from consideration, with great practical advantage. But as Frege in effect pointed out,[1] a calculus of this kind is a game, and as a game is not logic. To interpret it as a logic is to interpret the marks as symbols and formulae, and the rules of play as rules of inference. But if my argument is correct, inferring and thinking that something is the case are not actions or activities, and it follows that if inferences are thought of as valid or invalid according to their conformity to or contravention of logical principles, which principles are then thought of as rules of inference, these rules or principles cannot be rules or principles of conduct, even of mental conduct.

---

[1] In *The Foundations of Arithmetic,* vol. ii, section 86 ff.

3

LOGICAL APPRAISAL AND THE
APPRAISAL OF BELIEF

3.1. *Logical appraisal*

Though the psychological verbs of reason are not verbs of action, belonging to Group (4) rather than Group (5) (see 1.4), and the logical verbs designate relations between things that can be said, items belonging to Groups (1), (2), and (3), an important idea can be salvaged from the wreck of the practical conception of reason. It is the idea of a close connection between the logical and psychological verbs, mediated through a third nuclear group of concepts of reason: the concepts of logical appraisal, criticism, and evaluation.

In the following two lists, '*p*' and '*q*' are, as usual, proposition variables, and the items in List A represent, let us suppose, truths of reason, whether deductive, inductive, or what not:

List A

(1) '*p*' implies '*q*'.

(2) If *p* then *q*.

(3) '*q*' follows from '*p*'.

(4) '*p*' is inconsistent with '*not-q*'.

List B

(1) The argument or inference from '*p*' to '*q*' is valid not invalid, sound not unsound, acceptable not unacceptable, a good not a bad argument.

(2) From the fact that *p* one can (legitimately or correctly) argue, infer, deduce, or conclude that *q*.

(3) The fact that *p* is a (conclusive) reason for thinking that *q*.

(4) The fact that *p* justifies the belief that *q*.

(5) It's right not wrong, correct not mistaken, to think that *q*, because *p*.

(6) It is inconsistent to think that *p* and at the same time think that *not-q*.

There are two questions: first, are the items of List A distinguishable from those of List B; and if so, second, is there any necessary connection between them? The *prima facie* answer to both of these questions is 'Yes'. List A contains truths of reason, some instances of which would be analytic, A1, e.g., asserting that the logical relation of implication holds between two propositions or propositional formulae. In contrast, List B is a list of appraisals, which contain both evaluative and psychological concepts, the evaluative concepts being used in the appraisal of what the psychological concepts designate, actual or possible arguments, inferences, deductions, conclusions, or beliefs: under this interpretation, B1, for instance, could be regarded as a normative rule, a rule of inference. Yet between the items in these two lists there seems to be a strong logical connection: if A1–4, then B1 and B6, and if A1–4 and it is the case that *p* (whether this is itself analytic, descriptive, or evaluative), then B2–5. This *prima facie* answer gives a partial elucidation of the view that logical principles are 'Laws of Thought': they are not psychological laws, but principles necessarily having a normative bearing on the psychological states of people.

3.2. *Philosophical obstacles: the problem of theoretical reason*
Subject to some qualifications to be introduced later, in this chapter and the next, this answer seems to me to be correct, and I shall accordingly refer to B1–6 as evaluative or normative implications of A1–4; but some influential philosophical dogmas are obstacles to the acceptance of this idea. My claim could be summarised, somewhat clumsily, as follows: truths of reason,

including analytic and logical truths, have implications that are psychologically normative and substantive. Concentrating first on the psychological, then on the normative, and then on the substantive, aspect of the alleged implications, we can identify three obstacles. First, 'anti-psychologism' in some of its forms contends that logical and psychological matters are logically independent. Second, the modern generalised version (subscribed to by Hare, for instance) of Hume's claim that 'ought' cannot be deduced from 'is' and of Moore's claim that naturalism is fallacious, namely, the doctrine of what can be called 'the autonomy of values' or 'the autonomy of normative discourse',[1] contends that logical and normative matters are logically independent, in the sense that categorical value-judgments, normative or prescriptive utterances, appraisals, or critical judgments, do not logically follow from analytic (or descriptive) statements. Third, the view that logical truths, being analytic or tautologous, are non-substantive in the sense that they say nothing, rule out nothing, are compatible with any possible state of affairs, embraces the other two and seems to be involved in any rigorous empiricist consideration of the relations of Lists A and B.

I shall assume that my characterisation of the items in List A would be generally accepted: as truths of reason, including analytic truths and truths of formal logic, they essentially contain neither evaluative nor psychological concepts. In that case, these dogmas will put us under pressure either to agree to the connections between List A and List B and to deny the differences, i.e. to deny that B1–6 really are appraisals of psychological matters, or to agree to the differences and deny the connections. To get the best of both worlds, it could be maintained that the items in List B are ambiguous: to whatever extent logic contains statements like B1 they are to be construed as indistinguishable from statements of the kind in List A; but outside logic statements like B1–6 are or can be genuine appraisals of people's arguments, inferences, and beliefs, but are then logically independent of statements like A1–4.

My task, then, is to show how, as genuine, substantive appraisals of psychological factors such as people's inferences and beliefs, B1–6 are nevertheless implications of A1–4, i.e. of non-evaluative, non-psychological, and sometimes analytic statements of logical relations between propositions. That they are implications of

[1] As P. Taylor calls it in his book *Normative Discourse* (p. 255).

logical truths I take to be the chief insight of the theoretical conception of reason. That they are appraisals of psychological factors I take to be the chief insight of the practical conception of reason. The central philosophical problem in giving an adequate account of theoretical reason is: how is it possible for both of these things to be true? I shall start by considering the way in which B1–6 are appraisals of psychological factors.

3.3. *Appraisal of beliefs and inferences*

Even the simple platitude that people's inferences and beliefs can be appraised, criticised, and evaluated, and not from a moral or aesthetic point of view but from what we can provisionally call a logical point of view, seems to run counter to some common philosophical assumptions. Such evaluative words as 'good', 'bad', 'right', 'wrong', and 'ought' are so important in ethics and aesthetics that value-judgments have sometimes been thought to be essentially judgments of moral or aesthetic value, or to be peculiarly, or at least fundamentally, appraisals of categories of things central to ethics, such as actions, or to be necessarily tied to kinds of appraisal important or essential in these fields. One such assumption is what we might call 'the teleological idea of value', the idea that anything that is good or bad, justified or unjustified, is so either as a means or as an end. Another has this consequence, that the word 'criticism', unqualified, is used to mean moral or aesthetic criticism, so that the relation between logic and criticism is thought to be determined by the relation between logic on the one hand and morals and aesthetics on the other.[1] Another, which is perhaps partly a consequence of the view that moral evaluation is essentially of action, is that evaluation essentially guides actions or (presumably on the assumption that choosing or what is chosen is always itself an action) choices.[2] None of these things is true of the appraisals in List B.

Let us for the moment concentrate on B3. In my earlier rough and ready account of the concept of reason it was suggested that the terms of the relation of *being a reason for* are the premises and conclusion of an argument, or what can be inferred and what it can be inferred from: in a word, propositions. As my list indicates,

[1] See, e.g., the chapter called 'Logic and Critical Evaluation' in Cohen and Nagel's *Introduction to Logic and Scientific Method*.
[2] See what seems to be at least a fairly firm commitment to these ideas in Hare, op. cit., esp. pp. 1–3, 101–9, 127–36.

these notions are closely related, but they do not coincide in the straightforward way suggested. What is said in B3 to be a reason is: the fact that p. What it is said to be a reason for is not the proposition that q, which can be true or false, but something that cannot be true or false, namely the psychological item: *thinking* or *believing that q*. The fact that p is a reason for the conclusion not in the sense of what is concluded but in the sense of concluding it, drawing the conclusion. What can still be retained from the theoretical conception of reason is just this, that the kind of thinking referred to in B3 (and in B5) is the kind distinguished in 1.6 as theoretical, the kind that can be involved in inferring, not the kind involved in deciding or intending to do something.

Hume's dictum 'Reason is the discovery of truth and falsehood', or at least the use to which he puts this claim in his argument that reason is theoretical, not practical, blurs the issue at precisely this point. Contrary to what his interpretation of this dictum seems to imply, the phrase 'a reason for . . .', when it occurs in theoretical contexts, is typically followed not simply by an expression for a proposition but by a psychological verbal noun to which the propositional expression stands as object. Such a composite expression is in Hare's language one kind of phrastic. What this structure implies is that what the reason favours or justifies is the psychological feature designated by the verbal noun: as in 'a reason for believing, thinking, supposing, feeling convinced, maintaining, concluding, that . . .'. This is true also of the phrase 'a reason to . . .'. Now of course things that can be true or false, propositions and theories, what somebody says, asserts, claims, or believes, are among the sorts of things that can be said to be reasonable, rational, or justifiable—and logical, where this is a term of appraisal, contrasting with its contrary 'illogical', not a term of philosophical classification contrasting with, e.g., 'empirical', 'moral', 'theological'. But words of this group can also apply to the psychological items already identified, as in 'It's reasonable, rational, justifiable, logical to believe, think, suppose, feel convinced, conclude, say, assert, claim that . . .'; and these latter locutions give the meaning of the former, not vice versa. To see what this means, let us compare the ways in which the expressions 'is reasonable' and 'is true' connect with such expressions as 'What he believes, thinks, maintains, etc.'. Suppose that what he believes is that there will be a slump next year. Then to say that what he believes is true is to imply that it is true that there will be a slump next year. But to say that what he believes is reasonable is not to imply that it is reasonable that there will be a slump next year, or (to put it more grammatically and significantly) that there should be a slump next year; it is simply to say that what he believes it is reasonable *to believe*.

Like the other examples in List B, B3 is an appraisal, but its normativeness has a double aspect, a double aspect revealed if we ask the question 'What exactly is it an appraisal of?'. There seem to be two possible answers to this question: the belief that q; and the fact that p as a reason for believing that q. Reasons for believing things can themselves be appraised as good or bad. Is B3 an appraisal of this kind, or of believing that q, or both? Part of the answer, the significance of which will be explored in Chapter 4, is that it is a condition of appraising reasons as good or bad that reasons should be the sort of things that people can have, i.e. reasons can be attributed to people as *their* reasons. As well as B3, we can have such locutions as: 'the fact that p is *his* reason for thinking that q'; and, '*my* reason for thinking that q is that p'. Unlike the latter case, a first-person present-tense attribution, the former kind of attribution, third-person (or second-person), is compatible with evaluating the reason either as good or as bad: such an attribution is in itself descriptive, not evaluative. Even when the reason is not attributed to anyone, we can also say, e.g., 'The fact that p is (or would be) a bad reason for thinking that q'; but this could not (except as a joke) be analysed into 'The fact that p is a reason for thinking that q, but a bad one'. If the fact that p is a reason for thinking that q, that reason may be evaluated as some reason, a good reason, a strong reason, an overwhelming reason, or a conclusive reason; but as simply a reason *for* something it cannot be a bad reason for that thing, but only a reason *for* it in the sense in which this is contrasted with its being a reason *against* it. A reason is necessarily something that favours or disfavours something else: an essential idea in B3 is this, that in view of the fact that p, reason favours something; as a reason, the fact that p has a normative bearing in favour of something. But the normativeness of B3 is not merely in the relation between the fact that p and what that fact is a reason for. Its other aspect lies in this, that what reason favours is necessarily to be favoured or preferred. It might be thought that if reason favours something it is still an open question whether that thing is to be favoured or preferred; but this would be to misunderstand the idea of reason. It is liable to be misunderstood in this way if reason is thought of as one psychological 'faculty' among others, one whose claims, therefore, could compete with and sometimes be overridden by the 'claims' of other faculties, such as emotion or desire. B3, in other words, is essentially an appraisal of the belief that q.

3.4. *Do appraisals of belief guide choices?*

As I have already argued, the connected concepts of inferring and believing are not action concepts; but there is enough in the doctrine that appraisals or evaluations guide choices to make it worth while to consider List B in this light. Choosing, deciding, and preferring, and what is chosen, decided, or preferred, are not necessarily actions, and sometimes, in inferring that, for instance, there will be a slump next year, somebody may be said to have decided that there will be a slump next year, or to have chosen this suggestion, theory, or hypothesis from a number of competing forecasts, or to have preferred it to those others, or even, perhaps, to have chosen or preferred to infer or think that there will be a slump next year. But these things are by no means always true when somebody infers something. The word 'accept' is more generally apt than 'choose', 'decide', or 'prefer' in this context. To appraise an inference as valid is to accept it, and to appraise it as invalid is to reject it. To appraise a belief as one for which there is conclusive reason is to accept it, and to appraise it as one against which there is conclusive reason is to reject it; and accepting it in this way amounts, under certain conditions that I shall describe later, to being prepared to say some such thing as follows:

List C
(1) From the fact that p I infer that q.
(2) I think that q, because p.
(3) p, so q.
(4) q, because p.

Now whether somebody, myself or anyone else, does infer or believe something, and so is prepared to say some such thing as C1 or C2, is a matter of contingent psychological fact. Someone can infer or believe something, validly or invalidly, reasonably or unreasonably, only if it could have been true that he did not infer or believe it. It is this that the notion of choice draws attention to: choice is always and necessarily between two or more possibilities.

The doctrine that value-judgments essentially guide choices can be justified only as a misleading way of bringing out this logical characteristic of evaluative expressions of this kind, that what they are applied to or predicated of is thus accepted or rejected from among two or more possible candidates. What B1-6 guide are, simply and platitudinously, people's inferences and beliefs.

3.5. *Pragmatic appraisals of belief*

Insisting on the psychological content of the appraisals B1-6 exposes us to temptations to ignore or misconceive their connection with A1-4. It is part of the point of insisting on their psychological status that, though inferring and believing are not actions, they can, like actions and other items classified by Hume as 'original existences' or 'realities' (see 1.4), and unlike propositions as such, make a difference to things; they can have effects, and in general, in believing something a person, as he or a natural agent in doing something, can do things that can be described and redescribed in terms that connect these things with the wants, preferences, and moral attitudes expressed or presupposed in our value-judgments of actions. In believing something, as in doing something, somebody may, for example, increase his chance of success, or upset his health. It is certainly possible to appraise beliefs and inferences from this point of view, i.e. from a teleological, or what I shall call a pragmatic, point of view. But, as I shall try to show, such appraisals are radically different from those in List B and do not guide beliefs and inferences as they do.

We can distinguish two sorts of case that fall into this class of pragmatic appraisals of belief, the distinction between them depending on the fact that with respect to some proposition q, believing that q (and, with appropriate modifications, inferring that q) is one of three, not two, logical possibilities:

(a) A believes that q.
(b) A believes that *not-q* (i.e. disbelieves that q).
(c) A does not believe or disbelieve that q.

The third of these possibilities is itself distinguishable into kinds of case that differ importantly; but for our purpose at the moment (c) can be regarded as the situation in which the person concerned has no knowledge, opinion, or information on the question whether q, because he has not considered the question. Sometimes,

and this is the first sort of case to be distinguished, we think that
somebody ought or ought not to be in this situation, or that it
would be a good or bad thing if he were, the implication being
that he ought or ought not to have considered the question, or that
it would be a good or bad thing if he were to do so: as when we
assert or deny, e.g., that what she did was no business of his, or
that he had no right to any opinion on the matter, or that it's of
no importance whether he believes or disbelieves it, or that it's
useful to have some opinion on the subject. Here the alternatives
are (c) on the one hand and (a) or (b) on the other. Sometimes,
however, and this is the second sort of case to be distinguished, we
think that somebody ought to believe that q rather than *not-q*, or
that it would be a good or bad thing if he were to believe that q
rather than *not-q*: as when we assert or deny, e.g., that it would be
a good thing if he thought he were cured, or would get through the
examination. Here the alternatives are (a) on the one hand and (b)
on the other. When we ourselves know that he is cured or will get
through the examination, we can strengthen such claims by saying
that it would be a good thing if he knew these things, or that he
ought to know them. But we may know or think that he is not
cured and still without inconsistency claim that it would be best
if he thought that he were cured: by thinking this he might (to
describe what he thereby does) ease his suffering, make his last
days more tolerable, lessen the strain for his relatives, etc.

In their most familiar interpretation appraisals of the kind in
List B belong to neither of these sorts. This might seem obvious,
because it might seem obvious that the distinction could be drawn
by saying that appraisals B1–6 are logical or rational appraisals
whereas those in the foregoing paragraph are moral, or prudential,
or utilitarian, in general teleological or pragmatic, or some such
thing. But to put the matter like this would be to beg the very
question that is the central issue in this book: the question of the
range of such concepts as 'logical' and 'rational', and in particular
their compatibility or otherwise with the moral, prudential, or
utilitarian points of view involved in the appraisal of conduct.
Prima facie, at any rate, considerations of a moral, prudential,
utilitarian, or in general pragmatic kind are not thereby debarred
from being reasons.

Appraisals B1–6 are not of the first sort distinguished because
they select between (a) and (b), not between (c) on the one hand
and (a) or (b) on the other. B3, for instance, is logically indepen-

dent of the assertion or denial that the question whether q should arise for anybody: it says in effect that between the alternatives of believing that q and believing that $not\text{-}q$, the fact that p is a (conclusive) reason in favour of the former. To put the point in another way, in terms of different kinds of criticism: if someone thinks that $not\text{-}q$, his thinking this can be criticised either on the ground that he has no business to have any opinion on the subject, or on the ground that the fact that p is a conclusive reason for thinking that q and thus a conclusive reason against thinking that $not\text{-}q$. It is perhaps partly because appraisals B1–6 ignore (c), the case made possible by the occurrence of the proposition that q in a psychological context, that the role of the psychological verbs in these appraisals has itself tended to be ignored.

3.6. *Things appraised and things guided: normative and non-normative appraisals*

Appraisals of the second sort distinguished, like B1–6, select between (a) and (b), but nevertheless these too are different from B1–6. The difference is essentially that pragmatic appraisals of beliefs do not guide those beliefs as the appraisals in List B do, because pragmatic considerations, though capable of being reasons for favouring, commending, preferring, or perhaps in a wide sense 'choosing' a belief, say the belief that q, cannot be reasons for believing that q.

Let us consider a very general form of appraisal or evaluation: 'In certain (specified or specifiable) circumstances, or in any circumstances, x is better than y'. The sorts of things that can be evaluated in this way, i.e. the sorts of things that can be values of the variables x and y, are many and various: we can say such things as 'Warm weather is better than cold', 'Feeling warm is better than feeling cold', 'Believing that you'll succeed is better than believing that you'll fail', 'This view of the valley is better than that', 'That picture is better than this', 'Making people happy is better than making them miserable'; and so on. Philosophers have explained, or have begun to explain, the meaning of such utterances by connecting them, in one way or another, with the notions of commending, favouring, preferring, approving of, or choosing x. Now in the required sense, commending, favouring, preferring, approving of, and choosing x are all things that can be done (in a wide sense of the word 'do') only by people. In this same wide sense of the word 'do', the examples just given of

appraisals of the form '*x* is better than *y*' are some of them
appraisals of things people can do, such as believing that they will
succeed, or making others happy, and some of them appraisals of
natural phenomena, such as the weather, or natural scenery, or
artifacts such as pictures. Consider now the question of what it is
for somebody to favour, prefer, or choose *x*, where *x* is what the
appraisal evaluates. When *x* is something that a person can do,
this question has a clear and obvious answer: favouring, preferring, or choosing *x* is, or is closely related to, *x*ing, e.g. favouring,
preferring, or choosing a certain belief or action is, or is closely
related to, believing or doing that thing. In these cases the
appraisal guides what it evaluates, beliefs and actions; and for this
reason I shall say that such appraisals are *normative*. But when
what the appraisal evaluates is not something that a person can
do, this answer is not possible, and there is no answer that is
similarly clear and obvious. Value-judgments about the weather,
or pictures, clearly cannot be said to guide the weather, or pictures.
Only people can be guided by value-judgments, and in these cases,
therefore, the doctrine that value-judgments guide choices would
have to be construed to mean that they guide people in doing
things of some description in which the items evaluated figure:
favouring, preferring, or choosing warm weather, or a piece of
scenery, or a picture, would on this view be related to doing
something of some other description such as *seeking* warm
weather, or *enjoying* it, or *looking at* the scenery or the picture, or
accepting the picture if it is offered, or *painting* or otherwise
producing such a picture if one has a chance; and it might be held
that appraisals of this kind, to be intelligible, must indicate,
explicitly or implicitly, or through their context, which 'choices'
within this range are being thus guided, as when one says, e.g.,
'Warm weather is better than cold for holidays, or for fishing, or
for growing lettuce'.

   This distinction, obscured by the general doctrine that value-
judgments guide choices, is important for our purposes because it
distinguishes pragmatic appraisals of belief from those in List B
(see p. 49). As I have already suggested in connecting List B with
List C, appraising a belief as in List B is closely related to accepting it, and accepting the belief that *q* is believing that *q*. But this is
not true of pragmatic appraisals of belief. On the contrary,
despite the fact that believing that *q* is something that a person
can do, these appraisals are related to what they appraise rather

in the manner that appraisals of the weather, or pictures, are related to what they appraise. Pragmatic appraisals are essentially of a type that guide actions; but since believing something is not an action, pragmatic appraisals of belief do not guide belief but only actions of some description in which beliefs figure, i.e. so far as concerns their function of 'guiding choices' they have the effect of treating belief as if it were a natural phenomenon, like the weather, or feeling warm.

3.7. *Pragmatic appraisals and reasons for believing*

This can be best explained in terms of reasons. I have so far left vague the notion of pragmatic appraisal; but it is clear, I think, that what makes an appraisal pragmatic rather than non-pragmatic is the kind of consideration, i.e. reason, on which it is based. What essentially distinguishes a pragmatic consideration is this: in doing or being something of one description, say x, someone or something, say A, may do something of another description, say y; and an appraisal of A's being or doing x is pragmatic only if A's being or doing x is valued because A thereby does y, which is valued. Here, both the value-judgment and the statement of the reason are about A and what A is, or does; but on what and on whom does the reason bear, i.e. what is the reason a reason for, and for whom is it a reason? In general, the reason is a reason that the person has who makes the value-judgment, and by implication a reason that anyone has who considers the question to which the value-judgment is an answer; for it is a reason for the value-judgment, i.e. a reason for thinking that it would be, say, a good thing if A were to be or do x. The 'choice' that this reason guides is the choice of the person who makes the value-judgment, a fact brought out by Hare's doctrine that value-judgments entail imperatives that are *self*-addressed. The reason is a reason for favouring A's being or doing x; and so far as that is the case, its relationship to what it is a reason for is not pragmatic. For it does not redescribe *favouring* A's being or doing x in terms of what someone who favoured this would thereby be doing. What is pragmatic in such a reason is its relation to what is being evaluated, i.e. A's being or doing x. But in general the reason does not bear as a reason on what is being evaluated: it is not a reason that A has for being or doing x; e.g., if one's reason for preferring warm weather for fishing is that warm weather makes the fish bite, this is not a reason that the weather has for being warm.

However, when A is a human agent, a pragmatic reason can be pragmatic not only in its relation to what is being evaluated, but also in its relation to what it is a reason for; for in these cases, it can be a reason not only for the value-judgment, but also for what is being evaluated, i.e. it can bear as a reason on A's being or doing x. If, e.g., I favour Smith's shutting the door, because his shutting the door would keep the room warm (i.e. because, by doing this, Smith would thereby keep the room warm), this reason for favouring the shutting of the door is also a reason that Smith can have for shutting the door. This possibility rests on a range of other possibilities, i.e. on the intelligibility of a range of descriptions of what Smith may do: e.g., 'Smith is shutting the door *in order to* keep the room warm', where this means 'Smith is shutting the door *with the intention of* keeping the room warm'; and this implies the intelligibility of 'Smith's *intention in* shutting the door is to keep the room warm', and this in turn 'Smith is *intentionally* shutting the door *in order to* keep the room warm' and 'Smith *intends* to shut the door *in order to* keep the room warm'. In general, if in being or doing x, A thereby does y, the fact that A thereby does y can be a reason that A can have for being or doing x only if it is possible for A to be or do x intentionally, and to intend to be or do x in order to do y. This is not possible if A's being or doing x is A's believing that q. It may be true that Smith's believing that he is cured would make things easier for all concerned, and Smith may know this; it may be true that he intends to make things easier for all concerned; and it may be true that Smith and others are for this reason in favour of his believing, i.e. think it would be best if he were to believe, that he is cured. What cannot be true is that he believes that he is cured with the intention of making things easier for all concerned.

The notions of intentionally believing that q and intending to believe that q are incoherent because, roughly speaking, believing is too much like intending itself, and too little like doing. On the one hand, intending to do x involves the ideas of thinking that one is doing or will do x, and thinking something involves the idea that what one thinks may not be so; and for this reason, except in the kind of case I shall mention shortly, we have almost no use for the expression 'A thinks that he thinks that q'. On the other hand, one can intend now to do something not now, but to-morrow, e.g. to repair the car; and any reasons one has for repairing the car tomorrow can be reasons one has today for intending to repair the car, i.e. for thinking today that one will repair the car tomorrow. Now I could certainly think today that tomorrow I shall think that there will be a slump. But if any reasons that I could have tomorrow for thinking that there will be a slump were reasons that I had today for thinking that tomorrow I should think that there will be a slump, they would equally be reasons that I had today for thinking that there will be a slump: thus my forecast about my tomorrow's belief could be only either a forecast that I should continue to believe something I already believe, or an admission that my today's or tomorrow's beliefs were under the control not of myself but of irrational influences; neither case could be described as one in which I intended now to believe something not now but tomorrow. All of this, of course, is compatible with the fact that it is possible to intend somebody else to believe that *q*. When I do something intentionally, my intention is not related to my conduct as it is related to yours when I intend you to do something and you accordingly do it.

There are ways of talking that may mislead us on this matter. Someone may say of Smith that he needs to (or must, or would have to) think that he is cured in order to make things easier for all concerned; and if this were said to him it might look as if he were being given a reason for thinking that he was cured. But this would be an illusion. We may say of the river that it needs to (or must, or would have to) rise two feet in order to flood the fields; but this would not be giving a reason that the river has for rising two feet. It would not even entail that the river *could* rise two feet in order to flood the fields, in the sense that this statement would have if, so to speak, a colon were inserted after the word 'could': it would not entail that 'the river rose two feet in order to flood the fields' was a possible description of what the river would do. Similarly, the statement 'He must think that he's cured in order to make things easier for everybody' would not mean that he must make true of himself the description 'He thinks that he is cured in order to make things easier'; only that, if he is to make things easier, i.e. in order for him to make things easier, in order that he should make things easier, it must be true of him that he thinks he is cured. However, when we are talking about people and their beliefs, it can make sense for somebody to say of some-body *else* 'He thinks he's cured in order to make things easier for himself': but this would only explain his belief, it would not give his reason for believing that he is cured; and in this respect it would be like saying 'He thinks he's cured because he's afraid of death, or because he can't face the prospect of being ill for the rest of his life'. First-person counterparts of such statements would also function as explanations of belief, as long as they were past tense; in the present tense, they would amount to confessions that the speaker did not really believe that he was cured.

3.8. *Getting oneself to believe something*

Let us consider a reasonably straightforward kind of case in which pragmatic considerations favour something that, in our wide sense of 'do', a person can do, but which one cannot have reasons for doing. The verb 'feel warm', like 'believe' and its nearest counterpart 'feel convinced, or confident', can take a personal subject; but one cannot have reasons for feeling warm, and in particular one cannot feel warm in order to, e.g., make it easier to concentrate on one's work. However, someone who cannot concentrate on his work unless he feels warm can have a reason for *making* or *getting himself* warm, e.g., by running about, or switching on the heater; and he can be said to get himself warm in order to make it easier for him to concentrate on his work. Similarly, though Smith's reason for thinking that he is cured cannot be that he thinks this in order to make things easier for himself or his relatives, he can have such a reason for *shamming* this belief, or for *making* or *getting himself* to believe it, i.e. for persuading or convincing himself that he is cured. But in these cases what the reason is a reason for is doing something of a description in which the belief figures; it is not a reason for believing that he is cured.

Nevertheless, the situation in which for some such pragmatic reason as this someone convinces himself that he is cured is not incompatible with his having reasons for believing this. In general, when somebody has a reason for making himself x, and so makes himself x, i.e. brings it about that he x's, there is always some means by which he does this, some answer to the question 'How did he make himself x?', an answer given in a reply of the form 'He did it *by y*ing': e.g., 'He made himself feel warm by running about or switching on the heater, etc.'. Sometimes, the $x$ing is itself (unlike the case of feeling warm) something that the person concerned can and does have reasons for or against; and when it is, the idea that he makes himself x is the idea of his doing something that he would not have needed to do if he had not had reasons against *x*ing or a disinclination to *x*, i.e. if he were not under pressure *not* to *x*: the idea implies difficulty and the need for effort. When the *x*ing in this kind of case is itself an action, as in the example of making oneself kill an injured animal in order to put it out of its agony, the effort needed is of a special kind, namely an effort of will, and it can then be the sole means by which the thing is done, as when we say, e.g., 'It was only by an effort of will that I was able to make myself . . .'. When the *x*ing is believing something, this situation is logically impossible: the meaning of the word 'believe' is such that this word cannot meaningfully fill the gap in 'I made myself *x* by an effort of will'. There is no 'will to believe' in this sense. The nearest approach to such a thing is in the kind of case in which someone, for pragmatic reasons, makes himself believe something that he has reasons for believing. The means by which the sick man could make himself think that he is cured would be by dwelling on the favourable evidence and perhaps ignoring, or closing his mind to, or refusing to consider, the unfavourable evidence. But the expressions here that indicate how he makes himself think this are expressions for actions or activities or their negations: 'dwelling on, ignoring, closing his mind to, refusing to consider' the evidence. He may accordingly make an effort of will to do these things; but not simply to believe that he is cured. For believing this he has reasons, e.g., that his temperature has been steady for the past couple of days. These may be bad reasons, or not strong reasons, and under the conditions specified his believing that he is cured will differ importantly from the kind of case in which it is through ignorance or lack of intelligence, not because he makes himself, that someone believes something for inadequate reasons. For if someone needs, by dwelling on these reasons, to *make himself* think that he is cured, those reasons cannot themselves be strong enough to outweigh, in his mind, the reasons (or, perhaps, the inclination) he has *not* to believe this. That is why cases of this description, unlike those of ignorance or lack of intelligence, necessarily cast doubt on whether the person concerned really does believe what the description alleges: the description '*A* thinks that *q* for these or those reasons, having made himself think that *q* for these or those (pragmatic) reasons' is of doubtful propriety, and suggests a non-central case of belief. When, in these circumstances, someone says that he believes that *q* and behaves as if he does, one possibility is that he is shamming the belief, i.e. deceiving others; another is that he is deceiving himself—not necessarily (in our example) about whether he is cured, but about whether he believes that he is cured. But it must be admitted, I think, that our concepts do leave a gap for the possibility that he does believe or at least half-believe this, under the conditions described. The concept of self-deception is complex and logically slippery; and the idea of belief is such that we have little use for the expression '*A* thinks that he thinks *q*', i.e., except in rare cases, if someone thinks that he thinks that *q* then he thinks that *q*, and the point of the first occurrence of 'thinks' in the quoted expression above, the word normally implying that what is thought may not be so, is lost.

We may say, then, that though the logical pressures exerted on the one hand by the concept of belief and on the other by the concept of pragmatic reasons are in general conflict, they do leave open a small range of possibilities: as in the case in which the sick man, in order to ease the burden for himself and his relatives, makes himself, by dwelling on the favourable and ignoring the unfavourable evidence, believe that he is cured. Even here, however, his reason for believing himself cured, e.g. that his temperature has been steady for the past couple of days, though perhaps a bad reason, would at least be a reason of the kind in List B (see p. 49), not itself a pragmatic reason.

3.9. *The thinking that makes it so*

The same general account holds for the peculiar kind of case in which in a literal sense 'thinking makes it so', i.e., in which the proposition that *q* is (or is likely to be) made true by somebody's believing that *q*. There is no need, at this moment, to emphasise the importance of this kind of case, when the belief that currency devaluation will occur, or that the price of gold will rise, seems itself to be a major cause of devaluation or of a rise in the price of gold. Let us consider a simpler situation. Confidence that one will succeed is sometimes a condition of success: a student, say Smith, may need to think that he will pass the exam if he is to pass. What I have already argued implies that Smith's reason for thinking that he will pass cannot be that he thinks this in order to pass. The peculiarity of this kind of case is this. Smith and I may both know that if he thinks he will pass, then he will pass. Now if he in fact thinks that he will pass, the fact that he thinks this will then be a reason for thinking that he will pass—but not without qualification; for though it can be a reason that I can have for thinking that Smith will pass, it cannot be a reason that he can have for thinking that he will pass. It may be that Smith has no reason for thinking that he will pass; but whether he has or not, the fact that he thinks that he will pass cannot be his reason for thinking that he will pass. Another kind of case shares this characteristic: if Smith is an expert on some topic, the fact that he thinks that q is a reason that I can have, but not a reason that he can have, for thinking that q. Part of the explanation why the fact that Smith thinks that q cannot be a reason that he can have for thinking that q will become clear later (3.15). The point to be made at the moment is that we have here one sort of qualification to my claim of a general connection between items in List A and items in List B, a qualification made necessary by the occurrence of psychological concepts in List B. The question whether the fact that p is a reason for thinking that q depends not only on whether it is true that if p then q but also on whose thinking is in question. Of two people, Jones and Smith, who know that if p then q, it may be true that the fact that p is a reason that Jones but not Smith can have for thinking that q: namely, when the fact that p is the fact that Smith thinks that q.

3.10. *Truth and reason, pragmatic and otherwise*

In my earlier discussion of B3 (see 3.3), I introduced the general notion of reason's favouring the belief that q, but the possibility of appraising beliefs from a pragmatic point of view compelled us to distinguish two ways in which reason could favour a belief: unlike reasons of the sort referred to in B3, pragmatic reasons favouring the belief that q are not reasons for believing that q. One of the most basic differences explaining the other differences between pragmatic reasons and reasons of the kind in B3 is that it is analytically true of B3, but not of pragmatic reasons, that if the fact that p is a reason favouring the belief that q, the better the reason the more likely it is that q; so that if the fact that p is a conclusive reason favouring the belief that q, then q. This is why C3 and C4 are so closely related to B3, and this also, therefore, helps to explain why in philosophical thinking about these matters the role played by propositions in these appraisals has over-shadowed the role played by the psychological verbs. But this and the other differences I have described between pragmatic reasons and reasons of the kind in B3, are distinctions, not incompatibilities. It may be true that q, and that there are conclusive reasons for thinking that q, and that there are pragmatic reasons favouringthe belief that q. More strongly, there may be pragmatic considerations in favour of the belief that q *because* there are conclusive reasons for thinking that q. But unless the claim that there were conclusive pragmatic reasons in favour of the belief that q were based on and so presupposed the claim that there were conclusive reasons for thinking that q, it would not be analytic that if there were conclusive pragmatic reasons in favour of the belief that q, then q.

3.11. *Logical appraisal and appraising the logic of something*

The distinction I have drawn between the two kinds of appraisal enables us to distinguish two ways in which an appraisal of something may be said to be a logical or rational appraisal. Someone may appraise, say, a tree, or a clock, or a dog, or an actress, and we can specify the kind of appraisal involved by describing it as, say, aesthetic appraisal; or by specifying the point of view from which the appraisal is made, as when we say that the appraisal was made from an aesthetic point of view. Sometimes there is a general word that can be introduced to specify what it is about the tree that is being appraised, as when someone is said to appraise the beauty of the tree; but this way of talking leaves open the possibility that the appraisal is not aesthetic but, say, economic, as a house-agent might put a commercial value on the beauty of a tree in a garden. Now an aesthetic appraisal may also be a logical or rational appraisal in the sense in which that aesthetic appraisal may be rationally justified; but it would not follow that such an appraisal was an appraisal *of* the logic or rationality of what was being appraised (e.g. the tree). The appraisals of belief and inference in B1–6 (see p. 49) are logical or rational in this sense, that they are *of* the logic or rationality of beliefs and inferences; but they are not only of the logic and rationality of beliefs and inferences, they are also *from* that very point of view, considerations for and against those beliefs and inferences being necessarily for and against a favourable appraisal of them.

3.12. *Anti-psychologism*

That concludes what I have to say about the way in which B1–6 are appraisals of psychological factors. In explaining this, in particular in distinguishing B1–6 from pragmatic appraisals of belief, I have already (and unavoidably) drawn on the idea of their close connection with A1–4. I turn now to this part of my thesis, that as appraisals of psychological factors B1–6 are nevertheless implications of A1–4. To explain and defend this contention I shall consider the three obstacles I mentioned earlier. The aspects of my thesis on which the three dogmas bear are so clearly interconnected that it will be impossible to deal with each obstacle separately in turn, but my argument can be regarded as divisible more vaguely into three phases, according to which obstacle is the dominant topic; and first, anti-psychologism.

Anti-psychologism has many forms. Some of these can best be regarded as policies for the establishment and development of the specialist discipline of formal logic, and as such they are not necessarily incompatible with my claim: e.g., the idea of formal logic as a specialist subject pursuing its own kind of truth, logical truth, logical truth being defined in terms of the essential occurrence of constants that do not include psychological concepts. It is clearly legitimate to limit a specialism in this way. But then it must be said that the boundaries of a specialism do not necessarily mark a logical gap between statements that belong inside and statements that belong outside those boundaries. The fact that an anthropologist describing a community would not in his professional capacity draw moral conclusions about the members of that community does not show that such conclusions do not follow; any more than the fact that a physicist or geographer does not draw tautological conclusions shows that the truths of logic do not follow from the truths of physics or geography. It might be objected that logic is precisely the subject that traces the logical connection of what follows from what, regardless of the more or less artificial boundaries drawn for convenience between different subjects; and therefore, if B1, construed as distinguishable from A1, really did follow from it, B1, like A1, would be a truth of logic, which it is not. My reply is that if B1 is ruled out as a truth of logic because it essentially contains psychological terms, which are not formal in the sense required by the definition of logical truth, formal logic is not 'the subject that traces the logical connection of what follows from what, regardless of the more or less artificial boundaries drawn for convenience between different subjects'; being 'formal', it is itself a specialism within the wider field of logic in general.

Specialist policies apart, we can, for our purposes, distinguish three forms of anti-psychologism:

(i) Truths of logic are not statements of psychological fact, and logical principles are not descriptive psychological laws.

(ii) Except for the fact that logical variables, e.g. proposition variables, are variables for which psychological terms and propositions can be substituted, truths of logic do not imply statements containing psychological concepts.

(iii) Logical reasons are not psychological causes.

My claim is compatible with (i) and differs from it in two ways. I am arguing for the relation of implication, not identity, between List A and List B; and more important, the items in List B, though they contain psychological concepts, are not statements of psychological fact or descriptive psychological laws but appraisals or evaluations of psychological items. The anti-psychologism of (iii) I shall consider later (4.12). What at the moment I want to argue against is (ii). In arguing against (ii) I shall be indicating the kind of implication I take to hold between List A and List B: to put my position briefly, it is that so far as the implication involves psychological concepts it holds in virtue of the meanings of those concepts and of those items in List A, and can therefore be regarded as 'analytic'; but the meanings of A1–4 are involved in a sense of 'meaning' different from that which is sometimes labelled 'content'.

3.13. *Content, meaning, and force*

The word 'content' is itself vague enough, but there are two uses of it, one narrow and the other broader, in which it would be true to say that the implication from List A to List B does not hold in virtue of the content of A1–4. The narrow sense is the one used by some formal logicians in explaining the way in which logic is 'formal': the form of a statement is determined by those words in it that have no descriptive or referential meaning, and its content is thus what it is in some sense about, its subject-matter. Thus the implication from '*p* or *q*' to 'not both *not-p* and *not-q*' is formal because it holds in virtue of the meanings of the formal words 'or', 'not', and 'and'. However, though these words have no descriptive or referential meaning (or content), they have meaning of some sort, and there seems no reason to deny that if a statement *contains* a word and its meaning that word and its meaning are part of the *content* of that statement. This is the broader use of the word 'content', and most of what are normally regarded as analytic implications, whether formal or not, hold in virtue of the content of the related propositions in this broad sense.

In this sense (and therefore in the narrow sense too), the content of B1–6 differs radically from that of A1–4. The subject-matter of the items in List B, what they are about, is inferences, arguments, thoughts, and beliefs; and neither these psychological words nor their synonyms occur in A1–4. How can it be the case, then, that it is in virtue of their meaning that statements that do not contain these notions imply statements that do?

One possible general answer to this question has been given by Hare in the course of his account of hypothetical imperatives:[1] an implied statement can contain concepts that do not occur in the implying statement as long as those extra concepts are 'added solely on the strength of definitions of terms'. Now this may be the beginning of an explanation, but is it no more than a beginning: the problem is how this qualification is to be interpreted. In applying this general principle to the problem of how hypothetical imperatives can be deduced from indicative statements of fact, Hare explains the qualification as follows: '. . . the imperative element in a hypothetical imperative is analytic . . . because the imperatives in the two parts, so to say, cancel one another out. It is an imperative, but, *qua* imperative, has no content; the content which it has is that of the indicative . . . from which it is derived'.[2] I shall later (3.19) give an interpretation of this last claim that seems to me acceptable for the relation of List A to List B; but its acceptability depends on not construing the appraisals in List B as hypothetical imperatives for, as I shall argue in the next chapter, this explanation of Hare's must be rejected as an account of hypothetical imperatives. Considered as a whole, and independently of the question of hypothetical imperatives, its implications for our particular problem here must also be rejected. Hare's explanation moves from the notion of analyticity to those of 'cancelling out' and of 'having no content'. But given these connections it seems to follow that if '*p*' analytically implies '*q*', then '*q*' cannot have any more content than '*p*'; and if '*p*' is itself analytic, '*q*' cannot have any content at all. On this account, then, it would follow that analytic versions of the formulae in List A

[1] op. cit., pp. 33–7.
[2] p. 37.

would have normative implications that were entirely without content; and in Hare's usage this would seem to mean that there would be no possible way in which these 'norms' could be contravened. But this (as I have already pointed out) is obviously false; so this account cannot explain how items in List A analytically imply items in List B. As we shall see shortly, part of the trouble here is with the idea that analytic utterances have no content in this sense.

Any answer of Hare's general sort would presumably explain the presence of both psychological and evaluative concepts in the implications of A1-4. If we concentrate on anti-psychologism in particular, and so try to answer the question about the psychological content of B1-6 in isolation from the question about the evaluative content of these statements, the most that can be done is to draw attention to some relevant considerations in Moore and Austin. Moore has pointed out[1] that forms of words like 'It is raining but I do not believe that it is' are in some way absurd or self-contradictory: there is an implication or quasi-implication between 'It is raining' and 'I believe that it is raining'. In *How To Do Things With Words*, one of Austin's chief themes is that the meaning or force of an expression is a function not only of its content but also of what it is used for in the sense of what it is used to do, i.e. what people do in using it. Combining these ideas, we could say that it is part of the meaning or force of the propositional form of words, i.e. any form of words that within the conventions of the language expresses something that is true or false (or, allowing for vagueness, more or less true or false), that its basic use is to express or state the user's belief, conviction, or opinion, more or less assured: thus understanding the meaning of, e.g., the words 'It is raining' involves knowing that these words alone, without the addition of the word 'believe' or any of its synonyms or near-synonyms, can be properly used to state, express, or communicate one's belief that it is raining. This connection between the propositional form of words and belief is, of course, a fairly weak one in this sense, that the references to 'basic use' and what such a form of words 'can be . . . used to state' are designed to allow for all the situations in which somebody may say 'It is raining' and not believe that it is raining: e.g. when he is lying, play-acting, practising his English, or uttering the words as part of a compound sentence such as a hypothetical, as

[1] *The Philosophy of G. E. Moore,* Ed. P. A. Schilpp, 1942, pp. 541-3.

in 'If it is raining I shall take my coat'. But though weak, the connection is necessary and non-contingent in the way in which any connection of meaning is necessary rather than contingent. Whether or not someone who utters the words 'It is raining' is stating his belief that it is raining, he and others understand them only if they know that these words are apt and linguistically sufficient for expressing that belief: in special circumstances, linguistic or otherwise, they will not express that belief, but in those circumstances the same will be true of 'I believe that it is raining'. It is to be noticed that in this way belief differs from other states of mind, such as hope and fear, that have sometimes been classed with it as 'propositional attitudes'; and that is why there is no quasi-contradiction of Moore's sort in 'It is raining but I do not hope (fear) that it is'.

The situations in which people can utter words in the propositional form without thereby expressing belief constitute in particular no objection to my thesis. My claim is that certain things about believing that p and believing that q follow from the items in List A; and the explanation of this, in accordance with the foregoing paragraph, is that though A1–4 do not contain either the word 'proposition' or the word 'belief', understanding the meanings of A1–4 involves understanding the variables as proposition variables and thus as variables for expressions whose basic use is to express belief. Since the variables in List A are either quoted or occur as components in a hypothetical, it follows that they do not represent expressions being used to express the belief that p or the belief that q. Just as the formulae in List A may be said to be about the propositions 'p' and 'q', so, acceptance of the proposition that p apart, the implied formulae in List B are about, rather than express, the belief that p and the belief that q.

There is another kind of case in which something is said that is true or false, but where it seems odd to claim that the saying of such words expresses the speaker's belief or conviction that something is so. Though the words 'I am in pain' or 'I think that p' say something that is true or false of the person uttering them, there is, except on the conceptual borderlines, no possibility of his being mistaken on that matter and so no sense in claiming that he is thereby expressing his belief that he is in pain, or thinks that p. I agree with this view, but it can, I think, be turned to my account. So far as these first-person locutions are true or false of the person

uttering them, they say the same thing, constitute the same proposition, as second- or third-person counterparts with the same
reference. But other people can be mistaken about whether I am
in pain or think that p, so that their saying what I say in these
cases can be regarded as expressing their belief that I am in pain,
or think that p. Now I could not understand the words 'I am in
pain' or 'I think that p' if I did not understand them as first-person
formulations of 'He is in pain' and 'He thinks that p', and in
general 'A is in pain' and 'A thinks that p': i.e., I could not understand them if I did not understand them as formulations, from the
point of view of the speaker, say A, of something that from
somebody else's point of view would express that other person's
belief that A is in pain, or thinks that p.[1]

3.14. *The substantivity of logical principles*

To clarify further what is involved by way of 'psychologism' in
my thesis, and to prepare it for full exposure to criticism from the
dogma of the autonomy of values, I want now to consider the
other obstacle in order to bring out the sense in which, as appraisals of psychological factors, B1–6 are substantively normative,
evaluative, or prescriptive.

The rejection of psychologism raised a question for philosophers: if the truths of logic are not truths about people's
psychological states, what are they about? For those who rejected
also a Platonistic answer to this question, the only acceptable
answer seemed to be that they are in some sense trivial or verbal,
'trifling propositions', about language or nothing. The latter view
is classically expressed in Wittgenstein's *Tractatus Logico-
Philosophicus*: 'A tautology . . . allows *every* possible state of
affairs . . .' (4.462); and 'Propositions of logic therefore say
nothing' (6.11). Closely associated with this is a doctrine that plays
a vital role in Moore's argument in *Principia Ethica* that naturalism is fallacious: in the words of J. N. Keynes,[2] 'The denial of a
contradiction in terms . . . yields merely what is tautologous and
practically useless'. It is clear that Hare's extension of logic to
include imperatives is compatible with these views. Just as 'It is
raining or it is not raining' tells me nothing about the weather, so
'Shut the door or don't shut the door' (if this is an imperative
tautology) tells me nothing about what to do. In confirmation

[1] See also later, 3.22.
[2] *Formal Logic*, pp. 119–20.

of this, Hare says, considering the idea that a principle of conduct might be analytic:[1] 'But if it is analytic, it cannot have any content; it cannot tell me to do one thing rather than another'.

Against these views we may set a complaint by Archbishop Whately:[2] citing an example of an analytic proposition he says, 'The . . . proposition just instanced, is one of those which Locke calls "trifling", because the Predicate is merely part of the complex idea implied by the subject; and he is right, if by "trifling" he means that it gives not, strictly speaking, any *information*; but he should consider that to *remind* a man of what he had not, and what he would have thought of, may be, practically, as valuable as giving him information; and that most propositions in the best sermons, and all in pure Mathematics, are of the description which he censures'. Whether or not the Archbishop is right about 'the best sermons' and pure mathematics, if truths of reason do have normative implications there is a clear sense in which even analytic truths are not non-substantive, a sense in which they do not say nothing or allow every possible state of affairs. Using the apt description 'logical principles' to cover the items in both List A and List B, we can say that, as truths putatively about the way things are (i.e. A1–4), logical principles give us no information: they cannot be falsified, i.e. contravened. But as normative implications of these truths (i.e. B1–6), logical principles, though still unfalsifiable, can be contravened, since they can be contravened by our beliefs, assertions, arguments, and inferences about the way things are. B1–6 do not say nothing or allow every possible state of affairs.

More strongly and generally, if B1–6 are normative principles, it must be both logically possible for them to be conformed to, and logically possible for them to be not conformed to: i.e. the notion of conformity with these principles must be a contingent notion. This generalised version of the doctrine that 'ought' implies 'can' has no particular connection with freedom of the will.

Contravening or not conforming to B1–6 is not to be confused with denying or rejecting B1–6. Any statement or principle may be denied or rejected by saying or thinking that what it says is not so. B1, e.g., may be denied or rejected by saying or thinking that

[1] op. cit., p. 41.
[2] *Logic,* 2nd ed., pp. 91–2.

the argument or inference from '*p*' to '*q*' is not valid. But this is not to contravene it. As a norm or rule, B1 has what might be called a topic, in this case the inference from '*p*' to '*q*', and therefore the beliefs that *p* and that *q*, and it is on these items that it has a normative bearing. What can conform or not conform to it, then, are inferences and beliefs involving the propositions that *p* and that *q*.

To illustrate the distinction between List A and List B in terms of their connections with the modal concepts of possibility, impossibility, and so on, let us consider A4 and its implication B6. In A4 the word 'inconsistent' occurs as a logical relation word; in B6 it occurs as a term of appraisal. The content of the implication from A4 to B6 can be summarised as follows: it is inconsistent, and therefore contrary to reason, to believe inconsistent things. Now if '*p*' is inconsistent with '*not-q*', then it is logically impossible that *p* and *not-q*. But if it is inconsistent to think that *p* and at the same time think that *not-q*, it is not logically impossible to think that *p* and at the same time think that *not-q*; on the contrary, as is required by this normative use of 'inconsistent', this must be logically possible, though logically impermissible. The implication from A4 to B6 entails that though one cannot logically, one logically can, believe inconsistent things: this is not possible if one is to be in this respect logical, but it is logically possible, i.e. it is logically possible to be illogical.[1]

---

[1] These distinctions are obliterated in such well-known doctrines in the *Tractatus* as 'We cannot think anything unlogical . . .' (3.03), 'In a certain sense we cannot make mistakes in logic' (5.473), '. . . language itself prevents every logical mistake . . . we *cannot* think illogically' (5.4731), and 'Hence there can *never* be surprises in logic' (6.1251); and in 'The truth of tautology is certain, of propositions possible, of contradiction impossible' (4.464) there is an analogous tendency to draw no distinction between the logical modalities and such psychological states as certainty. More recent failures to draw these distinctions are common. Stevenson's whole programme of analysis in *Ethics and Language* is a standing temptation, and he commits the mistake in a subtle but definite form in the first of his Group I examples in the second section of chapter V, 'First Pattern: Method'. Max Black, in 'The Gap between "Is" and "Should"' (*Philosophical Review,* April 1964) writes 'When a man thinks that P and also that if P then Q, it is logically impossible for him not to think also that Q . . . To assert the premise . . . while showing signs of doubting or wondering about the conclusion would be an indication of stupidity, failure to understand, or some other cognitive deficiency': the conjunction of these two remarks having the odd implication that it is logically impossible to be stupid. For an example in von Wright's *Norm and Action,* see my review in *Philosophy,* vol. XL, no. 151, January 1965. See also later, 5.9.

3.15. *Conditions of inference*

B1 is more complicated. It says that it is legitimate to infer '*q*' from '*p*', or that '*q*' is deducible or derivable from '*p*'. Does it follow that not inferring, deducing, or deriving '*q*' from '*p*' would contravene this norm? Does the rule of inference rule this out as wrong or illegitimate? No, not in itself. The suffixes '-ible' and '-able', and the notion of legitimacy, function in this respect as they do in moral cases, where they connect with the notions of rights, licences and permissibility: if it is legitimate or permissible, or if one has a right, or licence, to do something, e.g., to walk across a field, it follows that it is not wrong to do it, not that it is wrong not to do it. This analogy is perhaps one factor that encourages the idea of inferring as action; but as I have already pointed out, the analogy does not stretch to the possibility open in the genuinely practical case, of seeing that one can infer something and then going on, or deciding not, to infer it. All that is true here is that if '*q*' is deducible from '*p*' it does not follow that it is wrong, i.e. mistaken, not to deduce '*q*' from '*p*'.

If, indeed, the normative implication of A1 is simply a permission or licence to infer, it may seem that contravention of any sort is impossible. But to the extent that A1 implies A4, B1 implies B6. Thus if A1 is analytic, B1 rules out, as inconsistent, thinking that *p* and at the same time thinking that *not-q*; and therefore, more strongly, inferring '*not-q*' from '*p*'. A condition of the implication from A1 to B1 is thus that these things should be logically possible: i.e. that 'A thinks that *p*, and at the same time thinks that *not-q*' and 'A infers "*not-q*" from "*p*"' should not themselves be inconsistent statements.

But a still further condition is necessary, a condition of the possibility not of contravening but of conforming to the principle B1. For B1 to license the inference from '*p*' to '*q*' it must be logically possible for such an inference to be made, and therefore for someone to believe that *q* because he believes that *p*. If '*q*' is a logical consequence of '*p*', someone's thinking that *q* may be a logical consequence, in a somewhat different sense, of his thinking that *p*. The difference in sense is analogous to the difference between two uses of 'entails' in the statement 'if "*p*" entails "*q*", thinking that *p* entails thinking that *q*': here the latter use of 'entails' signifies something like the obviously normative notion of commitment, as in 'Thinking that p commits one to thinking that q'. Now a condition of the intelligibility of these locutions, and in particular of the idea that someone thinks that q because he thinks that p, is this, that 'A thinks that p' should not imply or entail 'A thinks that q'. It must, in other words, be logically possible for someone to think that p and not only think that *not-q* but also not think that q. It is, I think, generally agreed that if a statement like A1 is true, i.e. if 'p' implies 'q', it does not follow that 'A believes that p' implies 'A believes that q'. My point is that if A1 has the normative implication B1, this does not merely not follow, it is inconsistent with that implication.

3.16. *Non-substantive logical principles*

I said earlier that the claim that truths of reason, including analytic truths, have normative implications is subject to qualifications. The most general qualification is the one that imposes the above conditions: that for a principle to be normative, it must be both logically possible for it to be conformed to and logically possible for it to be contravened. Certain logical truths do not have such normative implications, or do not have the full range of them, e.g.:

> (α) 'p' implies 'p'.
> (β) 'p and not-p' implies 'q'.

(α) is the 'trivial' implication or entailment that in effect says that any proposition implies itself; (β) is the 'paradoxical' implication or entailment that in effect says that a contradiction implies any proposition. The 'normative' implication of (α) modelled on B1 would not be genuinely normative: there could be no inference from 'p' to 'p' since thinking that p and not thinking that p is logically impossible, i.e. the 'statement' 'A thinks that p and does not think that p' does not describe a possible inconsistency attributed to A but is itself inconsistent and so necessarily false. (β) is different. It is certainly possible for someone to believe something that is self-contradictory and not believe some other thing which, according to the counterpart of B1 for (β), would be validly deducible from it. But as a rule of *inference*, any 'normative' implication of (β) would be vacuous, since it would permit any inference whatsoever from a contradiction: it would say in effect that in making an inference from a contradiction you can't go wrong. Yet since A1 implies A4, it follows that according to (β) it is the case not only that a contradiction implies any proposition but also that any proposition implied by a contradiction is inconsistent with it. In terms of B6, the normative implication of A4, it is inconsistent to believe both a contradiction and any other proposition. This normative implication is clearly incompatible with the B1 'normative' implication of (β). In other words, the 'normative' implications of (β) would involve the contradiction of supposing that a conclusion could be validly inferred from something that was inconsistent with it. It is not surprising that there could be no such normative notion of valid inference. For A1 to have the normative implication B1, it must be the case not only that 'p' implies 'q' but also that 'p' is consistent with 'q'.

We could say that (α) and (β) have 'normative' implications that are either vacuously analytic or self-contradictory, and thus not genuinely, i.e. substantively, normative at all. This is one way in which, even among analytic truths of reason, they are not characteristic.

3.17. *Criteria of substantivity*

However, they are not entirely peculiar either. Formula (α), for instance, covers the central cases of a group of analytic truths whose 'normative' implications are vacuous in this same respect: there is no reason to suppose that 'A believes that p' will be inconsistent with 'A does not believe that q' only when 'p' and 'q' are one and the same proposition. Given, then, that 'p' implies 'q', what distinguishes those cases in which 'A believes that p and does not believe that q' is consistent, and may impute an inconsistency to A, from those cases in which it is itself inconsistent? To put it in another way: given that 'p' implies 'q', what distinguishes those cases in which 'A believes that p' does, from those in which it does not, imply 'A believes that q'?

Let us consider an example. The proposition 'That figure is a triangle' implies both 'That figure has three sides' and 'That figure has internal angles that add up to two right-angles'. I shall say (perhaps, as we shall see, over-dogmatically) that it is logically impossible to believe the first proposition without believing the second, but logically possible to believe the first without believing the third. How is this?

The answer is that knowing the first implication, unlike knowing the second, is essential to knowing or understanding the meaning of the word 'triangle' as it is ordinarily used. It is for this reason that, given this connection between the implication and the meanings of its component words, no form of words could express the 'belief' that the figure is a triangle but that it does not have three sides: that is, there could be no such belief. Of course someone could say, could utter the words, 'That figure is a triangle but it does not have three sides'. But between the notions of saying and believing stands the notion of meaning; and a person does not believe what he says unless he also means what he says. I have already mentioned some of the ways in which someone can say something but not believe it because he does not mean it, e.g. play-acting. But in those cases the idea of someone's meaning what he says is a matter of his being sincere and serious, not joking or pretending, and so on. Now meaning what one says in this way is not sufficient for believing it. For given this connection between the implication and the meaning of the word 'triangle', someone who says and in this way means, i.e. says seriously and sincerely, 'That figure is a triangle but it does not have three sides' thereby shows either that he does not understand the meaning of the word 'triangle' or that he is deliberately using the word in a non-standard way. In the latter case he also thereby rejects the connection between the implication and the meaning of the word 'triangle'. In either case, though I can meaningfully and truly report his utterance in direct speech by saying 'He said, "That figure is a triangle but it does not have three sides"', I cannot, while accepting the connection between the implication and the meaning of the word 'triangle', identify his belief in the usual manner, by using his words in indirect speech; for if his use of those words constitute either a misunderstanding or a rejection of their standard meaning, so equally would my use of those same words in 'identifying' his belief as the belief that that figure is a triangle but it does not have three sides. His use of those words could not be said in my words to express the belief that the figure is a triangle.

I have stated this argument baldly, and it needs to be qualified by the recognition that there can be degrees of belief and borderline cases of the concept. But these subtleties can be accommodated without prejudice to my thesis, which without qualifications can be regarded as applying to central and un-problematic cases.

3.18. *The non-substantivity of errors of meaning*

In his *Examination of Sir William Hamilton's Philosophy*[1] Mill distinguishes 'two properties of circles', one 'connoted by the name' the other 'recondite' and 'discovered by mathematicians', not part of the meaning of the word 'circle'. My distinction between the two implications of something's being a triangle is analogous to Mill's, and its effect is similar to Mill's consequent distinction between real and apparent inference. However, Mill seems to align this distinction with the distinction between deductive and inductive reasoning, and so to conclude that mathematics is inductive. The more characteristic view of later philosophers is that mathematics is deductive, but this view often shares with Mill the common doctrine that what can be deduced from a premise must be in his sense part of its meaning. We can see here, in fact, the linguistic conception of reason making a minimal concession to the idea that analytic truths have normative implications: principles of (deductive) inference are verbal in the sense that the norms implied by analytic truths are linguistic rules, so that when contravention is mistaken and not deliberate it involves a verbal error and entails that the person concerned does not understand the meanings of some of the words in the statements and arguments in question.

The concession is minimal, and consistent with the idea that analytic principles are non-substantive, because errors of meaning, and in general linguistic mistakes, including mistakes of grammar and mere slips of the tongue, are comparatively trivial and superficial, not errors of substance. What, then, is the notion of a substantive mistake here, by comparison with which a misunderstanding of meaning is 'merely verbal'? The obvious contrast, in the light of the foregoing argument, is between a mistake in *saying* and a mistake in *thinking*. It is not denied that using a word wrongly can have important consequences: it can, because it can mislead others into making mistakes of substance. But the person so misusing the word is not thereby himself misled. If my wife says to me, 'The tank of the car is leaking', meaning by that that the carburettor is leaking, and I do not know that she has used the word wrongly, I may as a result make a mistake of substance, a mistake of fact: I may believe what is in fact false,

---

[1] 5th ed., 1878, ch. XIX, 'Reasoning', p. 444.

that the tank is leaking. But if so, what I believe is not what she believes, though we may use the same words to express our beliefs. Her misunderstanding of the meaning of the word 'tank' is precisely one in which she misuses the word 'tank' to refer to the carburettor, one in which, as we might say, she *said* 'tank' but *meant* 'carburettor', one in which, as we might also say, she *said* 'tank' but was *thinking of* the carburettor. She might, of course, also have false factual beliefs about, say, the function of what she mistakenly calls the tank; but to whatever extent this circumstance casts doubt on the correctness of refusing to describe her as believing that the tank was leaking, it casts doubt to the same extent on the correctness of describing her mistake as a misunderstanding of the meaning of the word 'tank' rather than as a misunderstanding of the function of what she calls the tank. This example is only one of a whole range of possible cases, and it lies between the extremely trivial at one end, such as slips of the tongue, and the more important at the other, where the misunderstanding of meaning is so radical that a person does not merely mean something different from what he says but rather means nothing at all, so that no belief whatsoever can be attributed to him as what his words mis-express. But if (apart from what for us is the irrelevant belief that he does mean something) no belief at all can be attributed to him in these circumstances, it remains true that his mistake is not substantive in the relevant sense: his belief is not mistaken.

The notion of misunderstanding something, including the meaning of a word, is one that admits of degrees: one's understanding can be partial or full, as one's grasp can be adequate or faltering. One reason for this is that understanding something is a capacity that can be exercised in many different ways, in the form of many different skills, and the degree of someone's understanding is a function of the number and type of such skills that he possesses. Thus between total failure to understand the meaning of a word and a full and complete understanding there is a continuum of intermediate cases differing only in degree. If the word is descriptive, like 'triangle', one essential aspect of understanding its meaning is the ability to recognise those items or characteristics that the word describes, i.e., in this example, to identify triangles when one sees them; and more particularly, to recognise and identify them as triangles, i.e. to say that they are triangles, or to agree with somebody else who says that they are, and so to think that they are. Another essential aspect, which would often, in practice, be difficult to distinguish from the first, is seeing some of the logical relations of statements employing the word, e.g., seeing that 'This is a triangle' implies 'This has three angles' and 'This has three sides'. Since there are degrees of understanding, seeing other implications may be included among the tests of whether someone fully or adequately understands the meaning of the word, e.g. the implication 'This has internal angles that add up to two right-angles'; and my example, therefore, may have been over-dogmatic in this way. But my argument is that if seeing all the logical relations of statements employing the word were included, it would be logically impossible for anyone to have inconsistent beliefs, or, therefore, to make valid or invalid inferences. In other words, the possibility of logical appraisal of thinking and reasoning requires a notion of understanding the meaning of a word that stops short of including knowledge of all the logical relations involved. In that case, contravention of a logical principle can be a mistake of substance and involve mistaken beliefs; and if the beliefs are themselves factual or empirical, the mistake in logic will involve a mistake that is substantive in being an empirical or factual mistake. For example, someone who believes that the figure is a triangle and also that its internal angles do not add up to two right-angles has at least one belief that is mistaken in fact. Logical principles really are in this way substantive laws of thought, not simply rules of language.

All of this may be accepted, I think, without prejudice to the doctrine that analytic truths are 'true in virtue of their meaning'. It is, indeed, this doctrine, acceptable in itself, that has been misunderstood as committing us to the aspects of the linguistic conception of reason that I have been criticising. That the proposition that p analytically entails the proposition that q does not analytically entail that the proposition that A believes that p analytically entails the proposition that A believes that q. Though the deductive logical relations of the proposition that p are relations that it has in virtue of its meaning, understanding its meaning enough for it to be truly said that one believes or disbelieves that p does not involve knowing what all its logical relations are. This is why, though the items in List B are substantive norms, i.e. norms that can be contravened, it does not follow from this that they are not analytic.

3.19. *Belief and the autonomy of values*

I have argued that the 'psychologism' in my thesis that B1–6 follow from the logical relation statements A1–4 is unobjectionable because the terms of the relations in A1–4 are propositions and it is the basic function of the propositional form of words to express the psychological state of belief. I have argued also that with regard to the states of mind designated by their psychological verbs 'infer' and 'believe' B1–6 are substantive appraisals and thus, in the sense clarified, substantively normative. What remains to be done is to confront the obstacle of the doctrine of the autonomy of values and see how, though substantive and evaluative, B1–6 nevertheless follow from the analytic and non-evaluative A1–4. As we shall see, the solution of the problem lies in the concept logically carried into List B by the concept of proposition involved in List A, namely, the concept of belief.

We can start from the following objection.[1] In accepting something of the sort in A1–4, it might be contended, we in no way commit ourselves to any evaluation of anybody's arguments, inferences or beliefs. For some people simply do not choose to be guided by reason, so that the step from A1–4 to B1–6 requires an evaluative major premise to the effect that one's inferences and beliefs ought to be governed by logical considerations, and this major premise is itself contingent. If someone says, 'I don't give a fig for reason and logic. You can logically appraise my beliefs and inferences till you're blue in the face, your appraisals won't commend themselves (or anything else) to me', there is nothing we can do—except recognise that the evaluative terms in B1–6 signify a choice of values that is independent of A1–4. The form of this objection is familiar from its use in ethics. That it can be used to drive a wedge, or reveal a gap, between A1–4 and B1–6 has been less commonly acknowledged. It has been less commonly acknowledged, that is, that the doctrine of the autonomy of values seems to imply that the connection between A1–4 and B1–6 is not necessary but contingent, and a matter of personal choice or decision.

Let us consider one specific form of logical appraisal, the form of B6, and its relation to A4. My brief reply to the objection is that

---

[1] This is the substance, to the best of my recollection, of a criticism made by G. B. Keene when I read an early draft of these views at the University of Exeter.

it is not logically possible to accept A4 and reject B6. The normative implications between List A and List B are of the type just
identified and discussed: there can be no such thing as an *inference*
from A4 to B6, because acceptance of the implication is a necessary
condition of understanding the words involved. Thus though
someone could say, i.e. utter the words, 'I accept that the proposition that p is inconsistent with the proposition that q, but I reject
the idea that there is anything wrong in believing both that p and
that q' he would thereby rule out the possibility of their being true
and a counter-example to my thesis; for his saying them seriously
and sincerely would show that he had misunderstood them or was
using them with a meaning different from the meaning they have
in my thesis. In particular, given the meanings of A4 and B6,
nothing could count as 'accepting', i.e. believing, A4 and at the
same time 'rejecting', i.e. disbelieving, B6: the assertion that
somebody accepted A4 and rejected B6 would itself be contradictory and so necessarily false.

3.20. *What is wrong with thinking inconsistent things?*

But this brief reply needs explanation, so as to avoid the impression
it might give of solving the problem too easily, perhaps by linguistic
fiat. Let us ask: what exactly is wrong with thinking inconsistent
things? Or, how is it that a logical relation word like 'inconsistent'
in A4 has an evaluative form as in B6? What I have already said
implies the rejection of one familiar explanation of these matters,
namely that saying what is inconsistent involves misunderstanding
the meaning of what one says. Another possible view, that an
inconsistent statement is objectionable because from it anything
follows, only explains the obscure by what is no less obscure:
what is wrong with being able to deduce anything from a proposition, and why should the unacceptability of this situation be
thought to be any more intelligible than the one it is supposed to
explain? The simple, obvious, and correct answer to the question
is that if the proposition that p is inconsistent with the proposition
that q, one of these propositions must be false, so that anyone who
believes both must be believing something that is false. This
connection between logical appraisal and truth is preserved in all
the implications between List A and List B. In characterising the
type of appraisal in List B, I pointed out of B3 that it is analytically true that if the fact that p is a reason for believing that q, the
better the reason the more likely it is that q, so that if the fact

that p is a conclusive reason for thinking that q, then q. The notion in B1 of the validity or legitimacy of the inference from 'p' to 'q' works in a similar way: as A1 shows, a necessary condition of its being valid to infer 'q' from 'p' is that if 'p' is true then 'q' is true.

3.21. *The normative implications of any proposition*

This simple and obvious answer is correct as far as it goes, but it does not go far enough, and failure to see this may tempt us into error: the error of supposing that the connection between notions of logical appraisal and the notions of truth and falsehood, in a word between reason and truth, is closer than it is in fact. We can bring out the nature of the error by imagining a persistent philosophical critic who claims to find my simple and obvious answer no more illuminating that the one I myself rejected on these very grounds, that explaining what is wrong with inconsistency by pointing out that an inconsistent statement implies any statement is explaining the obscure in terms of the equally obscure. We cannot, this critic may claim, helpfully explain what is wrong with believing inconsistent things by saying that one of the beliefs involved must be false: for this only raises the further question 'What is wrong with believing what is false?'.

There are three answers to this question that I reject as false, misleading, or unilluminating. The first is the pragmatic answer that believing what is false has bad consequences: I have already said enough about pragmatic appraisals of belief to indicate at least some of the things that make this answer unacceptable. The second is one that seems to borrow something from pragmatism— the view that belief *aims* at the truth: the notion of aiming here is clearly metaphorical and any insight worth preserving in the idea ought to be statable in literal terms. The third is that the words 'true' and 'false' are themselves words of appraisal: the difficulty here is that in the question under consideration what is said to be false is what is believed, and the problem remains how a negative appraisal of what is believed is related to a negative appraisal of believing it (rather than, say, disbelieving it).

What is acceptable in these views about truth and falsity can be extracted and stated without using these troublesome, controversial, and in this context superfluous concepts. The answer to the question is that the following basic principle for appraising beliefs is analytic:

(AB) If p, then it is right (correct) to think that p, and wrong (mistaken) to think that *not-p*.

This principle holds whatever the logical status of the proposition that p. Thus empirical and in general descriptive propositions, for example, have evaluative implications of the sort occurring in the consequent of (AB).

Indeed, it is this principle that underlies and is presupposed by the fact that analytic propositions of the kind in List A (see p. 49) have evaluative implications of the kind in List B: *logical* appraisal of beliefs presupposes appraisal of this more fundamental type. There could be nothing wrong, i.e. mistaken, in inconsistently thinking both that p and that q if this did not involve being wrong, i.e. mistaken, either in thinking that p or in thinking that q. There could be nothing right, i.e. valid, in inferring that q from the fact that p if this did not involve being right to think that q, given that it was right to think that p. It is in virtue of (AB) that logical relations between propositions have normative implications for believing and inferring those propositions.

We can see now how to acknowledge the intimate connection between logical appraisal and truth involved in the implications from List A to List B without falling into the error of supposing that the connection between reason and truth is closer than it is in fact. The notions of consistent belief and valid inference may certainly be defined in terms of truth and falsehood. But it is another question whether the notions of truth and falsehood come into these definitions by virtue of their connection with the notions of consistency and validity or by virtue of their connection with belief and inference. It seems clear that the former alternative must be rejected; the notion of validity, for instance, has no particular connection with truth when we use it of passports, wireless licences, or railway tickets, rather than of inference and arguments. The evaluative notions of validity and consistency are connected with the notion of truth only through the concept of belief; and the connection is mediated by the concept of belief because of the connection implied in (AB) between truth and the evaluation of belief. We can extract from these considerations a possibility that may be useful later, when we reopen the question how reason bears on things other than belief, such as action: the possibility that logical appraisal of something, i.e. appraisal of its rationality, presupposes appraisal of another kind, a kind not necessarily connected with truth and falsehood except when the something being appraised is belief.

The original objection from which this discussion started can be seen to be incompatible with (AB). Anyone who says 'The proposition that *p* is inconsistent with the proposition that *q*, but it is not wrong to think both that *p* and that *q*' is saying something tantamount to 'Either *not-p* but it is not wrong to think that *p,* or *not-q* but it is not wrong to think that *q*'. Now in general, if it is not wrong to *x* it does not follow that it is right to *x*: it may be neither wrong nor right. The force of the objection may thus be that thinking that *p* is neither wrong nor right, neither correct nor mistaken, whether or not *p*; as someone might claim that, e.g., eating meat on a Friday is neither wrong nor right. But this cannot be the case. The concept of belief, we may say, is the concept of something that is necessarily appraisable; it is logically tied to the evaluative notion of a mistake, to the notion of mistaking something, i.e. to the notion of its being possible to take something to be other than it is. The logical possibility of thinking that *p* presupposes the logical possibility of mistakenly thinking that *p*, i.e. of being wrong in thinking that *p*.

Let us suppose, then, that the objection is to be taken as implying that if it is not wrong to think that *p* it is right, or all right, to think that *p*. To see what is wrong with this we can compare the kind of appraisal involved in (AB), and thus in List B, with the kind involved in pragmatic appraisal. The most obvious difference is that no counterpart of (AB) holds for pragmatic appraisals of belief. I may consistently say 'He is sick, but it would be best for him to think that he is not sick'. I may even say 'He is sick, but it would be best for me to think that he is not sick'. However, this second statement signifies a defect not shared with the first. The truth of the statement that he is sick is compatible with the truth of the statement that it would be best for me to think that he is not sick. But since, if I say and mean this, my words 'He is sick' themselves express my belief that he is sick, what I say also has the force of a confession of failure, the failure of not conforming to what I take to be what is best in this respect: if I really accept that it would be best for me to think that *p*, not thinking that *p* would indicate a failure, possibly involving a conflict in which I try but fail to convince myself that *p*.

The kind of appraisal in the consequent of (AB) allows no such possible gap between evaluation and actuality in one's own case.

I may say and mean 'It is right to think that p, but he doesn't think that p' but not 'It is right to think that p but *I* don't think that p'. We have here, in fact, a paradigm example of the thesis about value-judgments put forward by Hare[1] and described in this book in 1.5. In the terms of that thesis, the value-judgment 'It is right to think that p' entails the self-addressed imperative 'Think that p', and assenting to the value-judgment, and therefore to the imperative, involves conforming to the imperative, i.e. thinking that p. As is well known, and as Hare sees, his general version of this thesis raises the problem of *akrasia* or 'weakness of will', for on a strict and literal interpretation it implies that there cannot be any such thing as thinking that it is right to x and not $x$ing. My restriction of this thesis to appraisals of the kind in (AB) implies that there is indeed no possibility of weakness of will here: for thinking in this context is not an exercise of the will at all. These really are in that sense 'theoretical' and not 'practical' appraisals.

In the light of all this, our original objection can be seen to be committed to allowing the acceptability, or at least intelligibility, of a position the statement of which would involve Moore's paradox. To say that there is nothing wrong with believing inconsistent things would be to allow that there is nothing wrong with asserting 'Either *not-p* or *not-q*, but it is right, or all right, to think that p and to think that q'; and thus that there is nothing wrong with asserting 'Either *not-p* but I think that p, or *not-q* but I think that q'. The concept of thinking or belief rules out such constructions as unintelligible.

Suppose, finally, that the original objection is construed as rejecting this concept of belief altogether. The account I have given of the implications between A1–4 and B1–6, and between the antecedent and consequent of (AB), fits the general solution of such problems given by Hare and quoted earlier (3.13): that an implied statement can contain concepts not occurring in the implying statement as long as those extra concepts are 'added solely on the strength of definitions of terms'. It is in some such way that we could explain the analyticity of (AB). But if so, it might be argued, we are free to reject the added concepts and confine our talk and thought in these matters to concepts of the kind in List A. My reply to this is that even this last resort is not open: for the 'added' concepts of belief and the appraisal of belief

[1] op. cit., pp. 18–20, 168–70.

in List B, are not logically independent of those in List A; whether or not such words as 'believe' and 'think' are used, understanding such notions as proposition, or anything that can be true or false, involves knowing what it is to think or believe that something is the case.

3.22. *The logic of belief: a schematic outline*

I have said that the kind of appraisal in the consequent of (AB) allows no possibility of a gap between evaluation and actuality in one's own case: I may say and mean 'It is right to think that p but he doesn't think that p' but not 'It is right to think that p but I don't think that p'; there is no first-person present-tense counterpart of the assertion 'He mistakenly thinks that p'. This distinction is enough to throw doubt on the idea that because 'He thinks that p' is a descriptive factual statement about his psychological state, 'I think that p' is similarly a descriptive factual statement about my psychological state. The connection between the assertion 'It is right to think that p' and the assertion 'I think that p' may then tempt us to suppose that 'I think that p' is itself an evaluative statement and not descriptive at all. In *Freedom of the Individual*,[1] Stuart Hampshire argues that 'I believe that p' is 'wholly normative': '. . . to announce my belief is to commit myself to a weak normative statement. For he who says that he believes that p is true says that he believes p *is to be* believed . . . for me "Do I regret that p?" and "Do I believe that p?" are, in the first case, partly, and in the second case wholly, normative questions'. This would certainly explain how there can be no first-person version of 'It is wrong to think that p but he thinks that p'. But it would also undermine the view I have been relying on, that 'believe' is essentially, in all of its uses, a descriptive psychological verb; and it would lead to misunderstanding about the meaning, to be considered later, of C2 (3.4). Hampshire's phrase 'wholly normative' represents, in fact, a serious oversimplification, and one incompatible with some of his other views. What I say when I say 'I think that p' can be true or false *of me*, and if it is true of me it must also, as a matter of descriptive psychological fact, be true for you to say of me 'He thinks that p'. Certainly you can deny what I say without denying that p is to be believed: for you can say 'No, you don't think that p, though p is true'. It is of course the case that if I do think that p I do not normally discover this

[1] London, 1965, p. 106.

fact about myself in the way that you might discover it about me, or in any other way; and this is an important feature of the concept of belief. But it does not follow from this that 'I think that p' is not a descriptive statement about me.

There is another misleading aspect of the view that 'I think that p' is wholly normative, another way in which it may be said to be descriptive. For the proposition 'p' may be a descriptive factual proposition, e.g. 'It rained last night'; and then the question 'Do I think that it rained last night?', which according to Hampshire is a 'wholly normative' question about people's states of mind, is for me indistinguishable from a question that is not about anybody's state of mind at all, either normatively or descriptively, but about the state of the weather, namely the 'wholly descriptive' question 'Did it rain last night?'.[1] I call this feature the 'transparency' of one's own thinking: my own present thinking, in contrast to the thinking of others, is transparent in the sense that I cannot distinguish the question 'Do I think that p?' from a question in which there is no essential reference to myself or my belief, namely 'Is it the case that p?'. This does not of course mean that the correct answers to these two questions must be the same; only that *I* cannot distinguish them, for in giving my answer to the question 'Do I think that p?' I also give my answer, more or less tentative, to the question 'Is it the case that p?'. This transparency is a basic part of the explanation how, if I do think that p, I, unlike you, know this fact about myself without needing to find it out or discover it. The explanation is that in finding out or discovering the answer to the question whether p, I thereby answer the question whether I think that p: these are not, for me, two distinguishable questions.

We can tie together these two objections to Hampshire's thesis. In virtue of (AB), the transparency of one's own present thinking ensures that one cannot distinguish the question 'Do I think that p?' from the question 'Is it right to think that p?'. This is the truth that Hampshire misrepresents. Again, it does not follow that the correct answers to these two questions must be the same, only that they cannot be distinguished from the point of view of the person asking the former question.[2]

---

[1] See my review of Hampshire's book in *Philosophy,* vol. XLIII, no. 163, January 1968.

[2] Recognition of the importance of the key notion of a point of view, as well as much else in this discussion, I owe to D. G. Brown's *Action,* section 1.9.

Let me summarise these arguments, bring out some of their assumptions, and develop them further. We are concerned with the relations between the following questions, where the first two refer to the same person: 'Do I think that p?'; 'Does he think that p?'; 'Is it right to think that p?'; and 'Is it the case that p?'. The problem is set by the fact that we are tempted to say both that the first two questions are one and the same question, and that they are different questions. The solution is that different criteria of identity and difference are here in conflict. I have already briefly outlined the sense in which they are the same question. We could say that where A is the name of the person referred to, they both ask 'Does A think that p?'. But from A's point of view this question is indistinguishable from the third and fourth questions, whereas from anybody else's point of view it is not. Granted that the idea of a point of view is such that 'the point of view of a person sets a limit on the questions that logically can arise from this point of view',[1] one way of settling the matter would be to say that the first two questions are one and the same question asked from different points of view. But this could be seriously misleading; for there is an order of dominance among these four questions, such that the answers are dictated from a certain source and in a certain direction. The idea that the first two questions are one and the same question asked from different points of view, for instance, might suggest what we could pejoratively call the 'psychological' account of belief, in which the first two questions (and for behaviourism the second question) dictate to the others: what is implied here is that the way to find out whether, e.g., it rained last night would be to find out a matter of fact about one's own psychological state, namely whether one believes that it rained last night. Whatever its scientific pretensions, this account looks suspiciously like mysticism. A similar air of mysticism is generated by the pragmatic view of belief already discussed: here the suggestion is that by considering questions of the third sort, e.g., 'Is it right to think that it rained last night?', and trying to answer them in terms of the effects of the psychological states of believing or not believing that it rained last night, one could find out the answer to questions of the fourth sort, 'Did it rain last night?'. Both of these views in their different ways misorder the priorities among the four questions. The truth is that it is the fourth question that dictates to the others, not vice versa. Of the two

[1] Brown, op. cit., 1.9.

points of view involved in the first two questions the first-person point of view is the dominant one. In other words, the first question dictates to the second, not vice versa; for the answer to the second question waits on the answer given to the first question by the person they both refer to, and if he has no answer to the first question there is no answer to the second question. The concept of belief, we could say, is in this sense primarily a first-person concept; and this is compatible with what I have already said (3.13), that understanding it involves understanding its application from a second- or third-person point of view. This compatibility is due to the fact that having the concept of belief (like having the concept of pain) presupposes abilities and tendencies to express belief (pain). In the case of belief, this ability is the ability to answer questions of the fourth type. Within the dominant first-person point of view this is the dominant question; for the other questions get answered only by someone's answering this question. It is the material question in the list, and the others are its shadows.

This network of relations constitutes a fundamental part of the logic of the concept of belief. It is this network that underlies and explains the views I have put forward and defended in this chapter, in particular the view about the relation between A1–4 and B1–6. If I am right, rejection of those views involves at one point or another a misunderstanding of the intricacies of this network and so a misconception of the nature of belief and of the role of reason in the field of belief, i.e. in theory.

3.23. *Belief and moral appraisal*

I have been talking about the appraisal of belief, and I have claimed that believing and inferring are not actions and that the appraisals in B1–6 are not moral but logical appraisals. The conjunction of these two claims might be thought to commit me to the view that logical and moral appraisal are independent, and more strongly that beliefs are not subject to moral appraisal at all. One familiar way of lining up the relevant dichotomies in accordance with these ideas would be as follows: moral principles, i.e. principles of moral appraisal, are concerned with conduct, character, and motives, logical principles, i.e. principles of logical appraisal, with beliefs, intellect, and reason. But this set of distinctions will not survive scrutiny.

For a start, if moral principles are principles of moral appraisal they are also concerned with beliefs, since to appraise, criticise, or evaluate something is to think it right or wrong, good or bad, better or worse. What I pointed out in 1.1 of practical judgments is true of value-judgments in general: their normal grammatical form is a proper indicative sentence, and their common conceptual context is the same as that of, say, descriptive or mathematical judgments in that like these they can be properly said to be asserted, denied, believed, doubted, inferred, and so on. Thus the proposition variables in Lists A and B range over value-judgments as well as judgments of other logical kinds, and everything I have said so far in this chapter holds equally for evaluative beliefs. I shall not argue this point further: philosophical theories that have denied that appraising, criticising, or evaluating something is holding a belief about it, such as the emotive theories of Ayer and Stevenson, have misconceived the nature of belief (e.g. by construing it on the model of a special case, or by failing to distinguish what is believed, a proposition, from the 'attitude' of believing it); and what is worth preserving in their views about appraisal does not commit us to these misconceptions.

In particular, it should be noticed, the basic logic of belief outlined schematically in 3.22 holds for evaluative beliefs no less than for beliefs of other kinds. It is sometimes said that people ought to do what they think they ought to do. This is a principle of a form already noticed in 3.9: if A thinks that p, then p. There are ways of interpreting it that can make this at least generally acceptable, e.g., as enjoining us, especially when we are arguing with people about what they should do, not simply to 'influence conduct' but to influence their conduct by influencing their belief about what they should do.[1] But to interpret the principle as a criterion of what people ought to do can be seen, in the light of 3.22, to be incoherent. For A cannot think that p unless it is logically possible that he mistakenly thinks that p; and both the question whether, if he thinks that p, he mistakenly thinks that p, and his question whether he thinks that p, are indistinguishable from the question whether p. The question whether A ought to do x cannot be settled, either for him or for anybody else, by the fact that A thinks that he ought to do x.

However, the sense in which, as principles of moral appraisal, moral principles are concerned with beliefs, is not that they bear on the morality of those beliefs. In being a principle *of* moral

[1] See also Brown, op. cit., 1.9.

appraisal, a moral principle must also be a principle of something else, namely, of that which we appraise in accordance with it, e.g. conduct; and it is on the morality of that that the principle bears, not on the morality of appraisals, i.e. of evaluative beliefs about it. In other words, a principle of moral appraisal is concerned with the morality of what is being appraised, not with the morality of appraising it. Its bearing on appraisal is normative, i.e. it functions as a criterion of the rightness or wrongness, acceptability or otherwise, of the evaluative belief, but it bears normatively not in a moral way but rather in the manner in which the items in List A (see p. 49) have a normative bearing on belief and inference, and the proposition '*p*' in (AB) on the belief that *p*. Thus with respect to the moral appraisal of conduct, a moral principle of conduct functions as a criterion determining the non-moral correctness or mistakenness of appraisal or moral belief about conduct. In general, taking up as correlative to the notion of a principle the notion of *applying* that principle to whatever it is a principle of, we can say that the cash value of the notion of applying a principle in this sense is to be found in the use we make of principles in arguments and inferences, so that those principles bear normatively on our arguments, inferences, and beliefs about whatever the principles are principles of. If the principle is itself a normative principle, say, a moral principle, it will also bear in a morally normative way on what it is a principle of, e.g. conduct. Such principles are, so to speak, normative at both ends, both at the applying and at the receiving end.

Is it the case, then, that moral principles cannot be *applied to* beliefs? Is it the case that though beliefs, whether morally evaluative or descriptive or what not, are subject to appraisal, they are not subject to moral appraisal? One interpretation of the principle already mentioned and briefly discussed, that people ought to do what they think they ought to do, is that moral criticism of people is in place only if they do what they themselves think to be morally wrong; for whatever someone does, if he sincerely thinks that it is not morally wrong any fault in his actions is due to a fault in his belief, and a fault in a belief, and thus such a fault in action, is a mistake, not a piece of wrong-doing, a shortcoming in intellect or ability, not in morality, foolishness or stupidity or ignorance, not knavery. The idea here is that moral beliefs, i.e. beliefs about the morality of, say, actions, are not subject to moral appraisal because they are beliefs not, say, actions. Against this may be set the view of W. K. Clifford:[1] 'It is wrong [and he seems clearly to have meant that it is morally wrong] always, everywhere, and for anyone, to believe anything upon insufficient evidence'.

Now it is certainly true that to criticise something as a mistake, though it is to say of it that it is wrong or has gone wrong in some respect, is not of itself to appraise it from a moral point of view. It may also be true that actions can be mistaken only derivatively, i.e. that one can do something by mistake only if doing it involves a mistaken belief; and this may make it seem as if the distinction between belief and action coincides with a distinction between items whose being wrong consists only in their being mistaken and items whose being wrong consists essentially in their being morally wrong. The concept of mistake may suggest this, but little more than that. We may still ask whether beliefs can also be appraised as morally objectionable or acceptable, and if so how this kind of appraisal is related to the idea of a belief's being mistaken.

3.24. *Belief and action: similarities and differences*

We can, I think, identify three sets of factors that generate the dispute, two of them seeming to favour Clifford's view, the other favouring the opposing view. The general assumption determining which way these factors bear is that if anything can be morally appraised, human actions can, for these are paradigms of items that can be morally appraised and perhaps the logically most basic items of that sort. Their essential membership of that category rests on their having certain features, some of which they share with beliefs, some of which distinguish them from beliefs.

(1) On the one hand, belief, unlike action, cannot be qualified by a range of epithets indicating that what they are applied to can involve an exercise of will: e.g. belief cannot be intentional or unintentional, deliberate or accidental, inadvertent, unwitting, or on purpose. The argument here is that to say that a person morally ought or ought not to x, or that it would be morally right or wrong for him to x, presupposes that he can x if he chooses, i.e. it presupposes that with respect to $x$ing his will is free; but since believing something is not an exercise of will the presupposition of freedom of the will cannot be fulfilled, so that believing is not subject to moral appraisal. On the other hand, belief is like action

[1] 'Ethics of Belief', *Lectures and Essays,* Ed. L. Stephen and F. Pollack, London, 1901, p. 175.

in two respects relevant to this question. (2) Believing that something is so can have effects, can make a difference to things. It can, e.g., be hurtful or helpful, advantageous or harmful. Within this set we may include without too much distortion the fact that believing something can be the object of people's pleasure or displeasure, hopes, fears, desires, and regrets. (3) Like action, belief may be attributable to a person's mood, emotions, or character: a person may believe something because he is angry, jealous, afraid, depressed, anxious, frustrated, bored, cheerful, or excited, or because he is selfish, proud, affected, vain, cowardly, benevolent, kind-hearted, generous, prejudiced, or malicious. Fools are not necessarily knaves, but they may also be knaves, and their knavishness may be the cause of their folly.[1] Connected with these matters are facts of the following sort: that thinking may be wishful and that one may be tempted to jump to a conclusion that one finds flattering or otherwise agreeable. One thing to notice here is that character epithets are less closely linked with attributions of motive than is sometimes thought. In British English (if not in American) to talk of what a person has a motive for is to talk of the range of items mentioned in (1), i.e. of things that can be exercises of the will: a person may have a reason but not a motive for believing something, though his believing it may be attributable to his envy or ambitiousness.

In (2) and (3) we have considerations favouring Clifford's view. Indeed, many of the key-words here, applied to belief, seem to involve moral appraisal of belief: as when we say that a certain belief is hurtful or mischievous, malicious or kindly. Is it not possible to appraise some beliefs, in a way that is obviously moral, as evil, vicious, or wicked?

Faced with these matters, anyone reluctant to give up the argument in (1) may explain them in either or both of the following ways. If we look closely at the matter, he may say, we shall see that it is never strictly speaking somebody's believing something that is the object of moral appraisal but, rather, either or both of the following: some action involving the belief, such as expressing or otherwise revealing it, or doing or failing to do something such that the belief is a consequence, as when a mistake is culpable; or some mood or trait of character to which the belief is attributable.

[1] See my article 'The Object of Literary Criticism', *Essays in Criticism,* July 1964, especially pp. 233–4.

3.25. *An essential limitation on the moral appraisal of belief*

The former of these may sometimes be true, but not always; and in the remainder of cases, the latter is sometimes true and sometimes half true. The general truth that is behind (1), but misrepresented by it, is this. The question of whether to do a particular thing can be a moral question, a question about the morality of doing that thing. If now we represent 'theoretical' questions as capable of being formulated in an analogous way, namely as questions whether to believe that something is the case, it may seem that these also could be moral questions; questions about the morality of believing that thing. But this is an illusion: the concept of belief ensures that the question of whether to believe that p is never a moral question, or rather that it is never a question about the morality of believing that p. For the question whether to believe that p is indistinguishable from the question whether p. Now this itself may be a moral question, e.g., the question whether one should peddle drugs; but this a question about the morality of peddling drugs not about the morality of thinking that one should peddle drugs. Whether or not the question whether p is a moral question it can be answered as a question about the rightness or wrongness of thinking that p only if the transparency of this notion of thinking ensures that these normative notions are nonmoral, so that the notion of wrongness is that of mistake.

It does not follow from this that beliefs cannot be appraised from a moral point of view: only that no factors peculiar to such appraisal could enter into the formation of belief; or more clearly, that the point of view of the person considering whether to believe that p excludes, by virtue of the fact that from this point of view this question is indistinguishable from the question whether p, the point of view from which the morality of that belief could be considered. Tying up this argument with what was said about pragmatic appraisals of belief in 3.7, we could say that considerations peculiar to the moral appraisal of belief could not be reasons for or against believing anything. Thus any such thing as moral appraisal of belief would differ markedly from the moral appraisal of action: for the moral appraisal of action is essentially shaped by the point of view of the agent, i.e. by the point of view of the person for whom arises the question of whether to do this or that; and considerations relevant to the moral appraisal of action must be, or be closely related to, reasons for or against doing things.

R.I.T.A.P.—D

3.26. *The effects of belief from the believer's point of view*

Let us see how this claim works out in the light of the kind of fact referred to in (2), that beliefs can have effects. How is it that the effects of $x$ing can provide the content of moral considerations when the question of whether to x is a question of whether to do something but not when it is a question of whether to believe something? How do effects escape consideration of this sort when seen from the point of view of the person whose belief is in question? If they cannot simply disappear, how must they appear in his field of vision? The answer is that from his point of view his belief that p escapes moral appraisal in favour either of the effects themselves or of what is denoted by the phrastic of 'p'. Suppose[1] that Jones thinks that his wife is unfaithful. Things that might in a wide sense be said to be effects of his thinking this, i.e. things that ensue *because* he thinks this, fall into various categories: e.g., he may beat her because he thinks this; he may be depressed or angry because he thinks this; he may be ill because he thinks this; and so on. Since his thinking this is to him transparent, these effects will from his point of view be attributable to his wife's infidelity; and the agent's moral question of whether to x can arise only either as his wife's question of whether, these effects being considered, to be unfaithful, or as his question of whether, she having been unfaithful, to beat her. In any set of circumstances involving beliefs, and in which one item is attributable to another, any moral question of whether to x can, and in virtue of the believer's point of view must, be seen to arise not for his believing this or that but always for one or more of the other related items.

This is true not only of the straightforward cases, but also of the peculiar cases referred to in 3.9, the cases in which thinking makes it so. Suppose, for example, that if people think that there will be racial violence unless immigration is reduced, then there will be, and if they do not, then there will not. The undesirability of racial violence gives no one, even in these peculiar circumstances, a reason, moral or otherwise, for thinking that there will be no such thing. On the other hand, in this sort of case the mere fact that it is true that there will be racial violence does not show that the belief that there will be is or could be justified: the fact that A thinks

[1] An example from R. R. Ammerman's 'Ethics and Belief', *Proceedings of the Aristotelian Society*, vol. LXV, 1964-5.

that there will be racial violence is a reason that B could have for thinking that there will be, but it is not a reason that A could have for thinking that there will be; nor could the justification be reciprocal, each belief leaning on the other in a self-supporting circle, i.e. in this situation, the fact that B thinks that there will be racial violence is not a reason that A could have for thinking that there will be. If A's belief has no better rational support than this, it has none at all: and in these circumstances it lays itself open to moral criticism of a different sort.

3.27. *Other kinds of moral appraisal: the moral appraisal of belief*

It is true that moral appraisal is essentially shaped by the requirements of appraisal from the point of view of the person for whom arises the question of whether to do this or that, i.e. from the agent's point of view; but the appraisal of items from this point of view is not the only kind, nor these items the only subject, of moral appraisal. Not only actions, but also motives, character, and people can be appraised from a moral point of view. Is it the case, then, that when I appraise a belief as malicious or timid or kind-hearted the element of moral evaluation in the appraisal applies strictly speaking not to the belief itself but rather to the person whose belief it is, and in particular to his character? What is true here is that moral appraisals of belief carry implications about the explanation of the belief, about why it is or would be held; and it might seem, therefore, that what one appraises morally is not the belief itself but the factors to which it is attributable, the reasons why it is held. Now sometimes a distinction of this sort is appropriate, e.g., when a belief for which there is some reason, and which may even be true, such as the belief that the Tories will win the next election, is held by some particular person or group of persons not for those good reasons but because of, say, envy or jealousy or prejudice. The distinction is parallel to one that can be drawn for actions: though the belief (action) itself, i.e. the belief or action identified in a way that is independent of its being the belief (action) of this or that person or group of persons, may be reasonable, or not unreasonable, *his* or *their* believing (doing) it is attributable to some personal quality that may be morally defective. Sometimes, however—and again there is the parallel with actions—the belief itself may be so obviously unreasonable that this distinction cannot be drawn. There may be some beliefs, e.g. that Jews are inferior, or that foxes enjoy being hunted, that are so contrary to the evidence that no one could have good grounds for holding them; and in these cases the belief itself can be appraised in terms of the personal qualities to which, if held, it would be attributable. When it is also hurtful or mischievous, as with the examples cited, the belief is morally objectionable, and can be appraised as, say, malicious, or cynical, or cruel, or more generally as vile, wicked, or evil. In this kind of case the belief itself bears those moral qualities because anybody's accepting it would be unintelligible except in such terms.

These are examples, and they should not be thought to imply that beliefs can be morally appraised only in unfavourable terms or only when they are to some degree unreasonable. Beliefs can be appraised as generous or kindly as well as malicious or cruel. Yet these epithets, favourable as they are from a moral point of view, are not entirely favourable when applied to beliefs: they imply some criticism, namely that the reasons why this belief is or would be held do not justify its being held. Now in the field of conduct the virtues of generosity, kindliness, benevolence, and so on, are contrasted with such vices as malice and selfishness; but between the two extremes are the virtues of justice, fairness, and impartiality, which signify the mean of doing what reason requires, not more nor less. These epithets are also applicable to beliefs: predictions, explanations, assessments, and estimates based rationally on the evidence may be said to be fair, impartial, or just. It should not surprise us to find that what is commonly regarded as the specifically moral notion of justice is closely connected with the general notion of justification, i.e. with the notion not of reason of this or that special kind but of reason in general. This does not mean that in its application to beliefs the notion of justice is not a notion of moral appraisal: the factors that justify a belief do not bear upon it morally, but the personal qualities required to accept that belief on those grounds may be or involve morally significant qualities of character or temperament.

Nothing I have said so far, I think, implies the falsehood that all beliefs can be appraised from a moral point of view. What then distinguishes those beliefs that can be so appraised from those that cannot? More clearly, under what conditions is moral appraisal of belief in place? The general picture that emerges from the discussion is as follows. Reasons for or against believing that *p* are factors that bear normatively but not morally on believing that *p*; these reasons put people under pressure to believe that *p* or that *not-p*, and people whose beliefs do not conform to this pressure are to that extent irrational or mistaken. But sometimes, other factors, factors that do not constitute reasons for or against believing that *p*, put people under pressure to believe or disbelieve that *p*, a pressure that can cooperate or compete with, override or be overridden by, the reasons for or against. Submission or resistance to pressure of this sort is of that general kind that marks a man as having certain morally significant qualities of temperament or character, good or bad. It is the presence of this kind of pressure that provides the necessary context for the moral appraisal of belief.

This is another aspect of the fact that logical principles are not 'trifling', 'empty', and non-substantive; another objection to Hume's doctrine that reason is inert. We must reserve for future discussion the idea involved in this matter: that reason is not only normative, it is also 'causal', i.e. reasons not only justify, they also explain.

4

LOGIC AND ACTION:
THE CONCEPT OF PRACTICAL REASON

4.1. *Reasons and what they are for*

In Chapter 1 I agreed with Hume that actions, as distinct from things that can be said about actions, cannot be inferred from anything, cannot be conclusions from premises. My argument there, and in Chapters 2 and 3 against the practical conception of reason, can be regarded as supporting what is supportable in Hume's position, namely: that inferring and the thinking (believing) that is logically connected with it are not action; that the things that can be thought (believed) and therefore inferred, though the sort of things than can be said, and therefore the sort of things than can be about actions, are not actions; and that the kind of thinking and believing most closely related to action, the kind involved in deciding and intending to do something, as when one says 'It's cold, so I think I shall shut the door', is not the kind involved in inferring. Inference, we could say, is essentially theoretical. From this position the sceptical argument is that therefore practical judgments, judgments to the effect that this or that should, ought to, or must be done, cannot be inferred or concluded from anything either; and this supports the thesis that such 'judgments' are not really judgments, but are, say, expressions of emotion or attitude, or imply imperatives, so that despite grammatical appearances they cannot be true or false. The principle of this argument is a doctrine about the relation of practical judgments to action, i.e. about the sense in which such 'judgments' are practical: namely, that if the 'judgment' that, e.g., one should shut the door could be a conclusion from premises so also could the action of shutting the door. As I have suggested, and as I shall shortly show, there is enough in this principle to pose a problem for Hare's attempt to combine an account of practical inference with the linguistic conception of reason. But though there is something in the principle, it leads to an untenable conclusion, a conclusion that is incompatible, as I have pointed out, with those aspects of practical judgments from which intuitionism draws its strength. The conceptual deformity that results from trying to think of actions as inferences, i.e. from combining action descriptions like 'shutting the door' with prefixes like 'I infer . . .', is conspicuously absent when one combines practical judgments with such prefixes. Shutting the door is not, but that one should shut the door precisely is, the sort of thing that one can infer, argue, or conclude, and the sort of thing one can think, believe, doubt, assert, contend, the sort of thing of which one can be convinced, sure, certain, or uncertain. Indeed, the sense in which these judgments are practical is not incompatible with their being theoretical in the sense of Chapter 3: as I re-marked in 3.23, nothing in that chapter rules out the substitution of practical judgments for the proposition variables in Lists A and B or in the account of belief given in 3.22. The point can be made clearer by comparing the kind of thinking involved in thinking that one ought to shut the door with the kind of thinking involved in thinking that one will shut the door when this is what one intends to do. When someone says 'I think that I ought to shut the door', what he says he thinks is something that can be inferred and something that, in thinking this, he may in fact have inferred, in which case he could have said 'I infer that I ought to shut the door'. But when someone announces his intention to shut the door by saying 'I think that I shall shut the door', what he thinks is not something that, in thinking this, he could have inferred: 'I infer that I shall shut the door' could not be the announcement of an intention to shut the door. If for this reason this latter kind of thinking is thought of as essentially practical and not theoretical, the title 'practical judgments' will be seen as a misnomer: as *judgments*, it might be said, these are essentially theoretical, beliefs that can be inferred from other things. It is equally true, however, that they are 'practical', i.e. related to action, in a way that, say, empirical judgments are not, a way that Hume's argument depends on. What is clear is that the inevitably crude dichotomy of theoretical and practical is no substitute for a close scrutiny of the relevant details.

In Chapter 3 I drew attention to statements of this sort: the fact that *p* is a (conclusive) reason for thinking that *q*. I suggested a close connection between these on the one hand and on the other such statements of valid or sound inference and of logical relations as that the inference from '*p*' to '*q*' is valid or sound and that '*q*' follows from '*p*'. But the notion of something's being a reason for thinking that so-and-so is only one specific form of the generic notion of something's being a reason for something else. Let us consider the relation in which *x* is a reason for *y*, and ask what terms this relation can have. The first thing necessary is to distinguish this relation from another, in the description of which the word 'reason' occurs in a similar construction, as when we say that something is a (or the) reason why something is so, e.g. the fact that the pressure is low is the reason why the weather is wet. With respect to the second term of this relation a reason is purely explanatory, and the two relations are different. As Hume in effect half-saw in his account of causality, the difference is not a disconnection, and there is no ground for supposing that the word 'reason' is ambiguous between these two uses. But we can mark off the relation we are interested in by saying that in this relation the idea of a reason *for* is contrasted with the idea of a reason *against*. Now: what terms can this relation have? The first term is always a fact or something asserted to be true: that *p*, or the fact that *p*; these are in general the sorts of things that can be reasons. On this matter, the theoretical and linguistic conceptions of reason are on firm ground: *that p* is something that can be true or false and something that can be said or put into words. A reason for something is anything that can be *said* for it, anything that can be said in its favour. But what items can we say things for in this way? What sort of things can reasons be reasons for? What is the range of the variable *y* standing as the second term of the relation? I showed in Chapter 3 that even in the most favoured case this term is in a different category from the first term: unlike the reason itself it is not *that so-and-so*, something that can be asserted or said, but *thinking* (*believing*) *that so-and-so*. This simple fact should prepare us for recognising that even this is only one of a much wider class of items that qualify as the second term of the relation. The answer to our question is that this term embraces a wide variety of psychological states and actions ascribable to people (or more cautiously, to rational beings). The phrase 'The fact that *p* is a reason for ...' can be completed by phrastics of many kinds: not only by verbal nouns of belief, such as 'thinking, holding, supposing, contending, denying, concluding, accepting, rejecting, maintaining, claiming that *q*', but also by verbal nouns of action, such as 'shutting the door, going away, having a drink, etc.', and by verbal nouns of feeling, emotion, attitude, and mood, such as 'feeling grateful, sad, pleased, being angry, impressed, annoyed, wanting, hoping, approving, liking'. To adapt something I said earlier: the conceptual deformity that results from trying to think of actions (or emotions) as inferences is conspicuously absent when one thinks of them as things that there can be reasons for or against. In the general notion of something's being a reason for something else we have a conception of reason far wider than that of either the theoretical or the linguistic conception. In particular, it should be noticed, the relation of something's being a reason for something else essentially fails to fit the strait jacket that Hume imposes on relations of reason in his suggestion that these cannot hold between items that are 'entirely different': the sort of things that can be reasons, and the sort of things they can be reasons for, are necessarily of 'entirely different' categories. As the linguistic conception suggests, reasons can be stated, and what a reason states is something that can be said for something else; but contrary to what that conception suggests, what can be said something for is not itself something that can be said.

The claim that actions and emotions cannot be conclusions of arguments or inferences, which is true, could justify the view that actions and emotions therefore cannot conform or be contrary to reason only on these two assumptions: first, that reason is exercised essentially in inference; second, that what cannot be inferred cannot conform or be contrary to reason. When we consider the use of the word 'reason' in such contexts as '*x* is a reason for *y*' the first assumption is seen to be arbitrary and the second muddled. Hume's habit of referring in one breath to both truth and reason, in the course of his discussion of what 'can be contrary to truth or reason',[1] is a sign of this muddle. What can conform or 'be contrary to truth' is what can be inferred, and this can have logical relations with what it is inferred from. But what can conform or be contrary to *reason* is primarily not *what* is inferred but *inferring* it: it is upon inferring and believing it that

[1] op. cit., p. 415.

R.I.T.A.P.—D*

the normative implications of the logical relation and of 'the truth' bear; these are the items that can be reasonable or unreasonable; when from the fact that p one can infer that q, what the fact that p is a reason for is not what one can infer, namely that q, but thinking that q. It is the relevant psychological items that conform or are contrary to (the normative requirements of) reason. Thus the second assumption is false even for inference, and would have to be rejected even if the first were accepted. But what of the first assumption? I shall put this in its place in the course of my argument.

4.2. Reasons, logical relations, and action

Given that the notions of truth and reason are distinguishable in the above way, it might still be held that the distinction is not a disconnection, and that the connection is itself enough to rule out actions and emotions as among the things that can fall within the scope of reason. For, it might be said, if one thing is really to be a reason for another, this relation must be mediated by a logical relation of some sort, as in the theoretical case, where the fact that p can be a reason for thinking that q only if what is thought, namely that q, follows from what is a reason for thinking it, namely the fact that p; and no such logical relation is present in the situation in which the fact that p is a reason for doing something, since what is done is an action, not distinguishable from doing it in the way that what is thought is distinguishable from thinking it, and actions cannot have logical relations.

What account, then, could this view give of the idea of something's being a reason for doing something, an account that would show that this kind of reason is not a species coordinate with reasons for thinking that something is the case? There have been two widely favoured alternatives: the idea of a reason for doing something is evaluative (e.g. morally evaluative); or it is the idea of a cause of doing something, a motive or desire. I shall return to this latter contention. It is enough for the moment to say of it that if it is incompatible with the former view, as it is sometimes taken to be, it must be rejected. The former view is correct. But, as should now be clear, that does not distinguish reasons for doing things from reasons for believing things. It can seem to do so only if the terms of the relation of being a reason for are crudely misidentified with the premises and conclusions of an argument, i.e. only if our conception of theoretical reason is dominated by the idea of logical relations to the exclusion of other essential factors. As I argued in Chapter 3, though not disconnected from the logical truth that the proposition that q follows from the proposition that p, the idea that the fact that p is a reason for thinking that q is nevertheless evaluative. And the considerations put forward then to show this apply equally to the idea of reasons for doing things. The word 'for' in this use as in that means 'in favour of', and contrasts with the word 'against' in the notion of reasons against doing things: reasons are considerations, things that can be said in favour of or against something, whether believing or doing a certain thing. Similarly also, if the fact that p is a reason, even a conclusive reason, for believing or doing something, it must be the case that the truth of p does not entail that that thing is believed or done, that is, it must be logically possible for p to be true, and believed to be true, and yet for anyone not to have the belief or perform the action that this reason favours.

However, to say this is not to answer the original objection that unlike propositions and other sorts of things that can be put into words actions cannot have logical relations, and that reasons for doing things therefore cannot be genuinely 'logical' reasons as reasons for believing things can. Is this view simply another dogma implied by the linguistic conception of reason? Can actions have logical relations? I raised this question in Chapter 1 and argued there that actions cannot have logical relations in the manner required by the doctrine that they can be inferred from other things. But in place of this rejected doctrine I am proposing the view that there can be reasons for doing things, and the question that arises, therefore, is whether actions can have logical relations of the sort required by this conception of practical reason.

Now, of course, words and phrases like 'implies', 'entails', and 'is inconsistent with' can occur meaningfully between descriptions of actions: e.g., shutting all these doors implies or entails shutting this door, and is inconsistent or incompatible with not shutting this door. But it will no doubt be objected that all this means is either that the phrastic 'A's shutting all these doors' entails the phrastic 'A's shutting this door' and is inconsistent with the phrastic 'A's not shutting this door', or that the corresponding statements or propositions or imperatives have these logical relations. But this is not, so far, an objection. It could instead be construed as an explanation of how it is that these logical relations can be attributed to those actions: the actions have these logical relations in virtue of their being describable in those ways. The objection could be pressed only by insisting on the distinction between actions and descriptions of actions in a way already introduced in my account of the theoretical and linguistic conceptions of reason, where the formula was: descriptions of actions, *not* actions themselves. Now in the present case such an objection can be interpreted as at least expressing an insight about the limitations of this kind of attribution of logical characteristics to actions. What is true of actions and descriptions of actions here is equally true of natural events and descriptions of natural events: the normative implications of these logical characteristics attributed to actions (or natural events) hold not for the actions (or natural events) themselves but only for what can be said, thought, or told someone about those actions (or natural events). If doing *x* in this sense entails or implies doing *y*, it is logically impossible for anyone to do *x* and not do *y*; but it is not logically impossible for anyone to say or think that someone has done *x*, or to tell him to do *x*, without saying or thinking that he has done *y*, or telling him to do *y*; and it is not logically impossible, but logically impermissible, i.e. illogical, because inconsistent, to say or think that someone has done *x* and that he has not done *y*, or to tell him to do *x* and not to do *y*.

Since a condition of this latter kind, involving normative implications, is necessary for the full and proper attribution of logical relations, or at least for any attribution of logical relations similar enough, for the purposes of my argument, to that involved in the idea of theoretical reason, we may ask whether there are any such relations between actions. It seems clear that there are, or at least that *prima facie* there are: for people can be *accused* of acting inconsistently. They can, e.g., be criticised for doing inconsistent things, no less than for thinking inconsistent things. But here we meet an objection similar in some respects to the one just considered. The differences between belief and action, it might be said, are so great that the notions of consistency and inconsistency cannot mean the same in the two cases. Two beliefs may be inconsistent, but someone who holds these beliefs at different times cannot thereby be criticised for inconsistency, for he has then simply changed his mind; he is inconsistent only if he holds the beliefs at one and the same time. But this condition is too stringent for actions: two inconsistent things cannot be done at one and the same time. We may accept this objection and turn it to account as follows. If the proposition that p is inconsistent with the proposition that q, it is inconsistent to think that p and at the same time think that q; but as was pointed out in Chapter 3, if this is so the second occurrence of 'inconsistent' here is normative, and it must be logically possible to think that p and at the same time think that q, i.e. it must be the case that 'A thinks that p' is *not* inconsistent with 'A thinks that q'. Similarly, if logical appraisal of actions in terms of consistency and inconsistency is to be possible, the sense in which two actions are inconsistent must of course not entail that it is logically impossible for both to be done. If the two actions must be actions of inconsistent descriptions, they must, therefore, to be logically possible, be two in the sense of being done on two different occasions, i.e., at the very least, at different times, or places, or both. But in that case, it may be objected, the two actions will not, strictly speaking, be inconsistent, only different: 'A's shutting the door' and 'A's leaving the door open' are inconsistent or incompatible only if they are descriptions of one and the same action, and there is no inconsistency if they are applied to actions done on two occasions. If we supposed that two actions could be appraised as inconsistent simply because they fulfilled descriptions that would be inconsistent if applied to one and the same action, inconsistency would be constant and unavoidable, since any action fulfils many descriptions, and on any two occasions it would always be possible to find two inconsistent descriptions of someone's actions, e.g. 'walking' and 'not walking'.

So far the objection shows only that fulfilling descriptions inconsistent in the above way is not what is involved, or not all that is involved, in doing inconsistent things. It is in fact a part of what is involved. How then do we distinguish between doing different things on different occasions, and doing inconsistent things on different occasions? The answer to this, and to the threat of the *reductio ad absurdum* in the last sentence of the preceding paragraph, connects many relevant concepts and could therefore be approached in a number of different ways. Suppose that a doctor has two old, incurable, and suffering patients, both of them lonely, without friends or relatives, and both wanting to die. One he kills, the other he does not, but lets him linger. What is involved in appraising this doctor's conduct as inconsistent? What the doctor did in killing the one patient will be describable in many ways: someone gave someone else a drink; an Irishman handed a red-haired Scotsman a half-filled glass; an ex-airman allowed an ex-soldier to drug himself on a Tuesday afternoon in winter; and so on. A similar variety of descriptions will also apply to what the doctor did in letting the other patient linger. Let us consider two pairs of such incompatible descriptions: the doctor killed one patient and did not kill the other; he handed one a half-filled glass on a Tuesday afternoon but did not do the same for the other. Why do we say that under the former descriptions his actions were inconsistent whereas under the latter descriptions they were not, but merely different? The reason is that the former descriptions, unlike the latter, are relevant to the agent's question of whether to do such a thing, i.e. they say something for or against doing that thing. It is not simply that there is something wrong or objectionable about doing inconsistent things but rather that its being objectionable implies that there is something wrong with either or both of the two items—something wrong other than their being inconsistent. This is simply a generalisation of the point made about the notion of inconsistency in 3.21.

4.3. *The basic logical relation in action*

This point makes available a further tactic in defence of the linguistic and theoretical conceptions of reason: actions can be inconsistent, it might be said, not in themselves but only in virtue of the inconsistency of the practical judgments or principles they can be regarded as conforming to, e.g. the judgments or principles that a doctor should kill patients who want to die and who are old, incurable, lonely, and suffering, and that a doctor should not kill such patients. Again, however, this is so far only a possible explanation of the role played by the notions of consistency and inconsistency in the appraisal of actions. It becomes unacceptable if it is offered as an objection, i.e. as showing that 'strictly speaking' only beliefs about, or principles, judgments, or descriptions of action, not actions themselves, can be consistent or inconsistent. What must be conceded to the objection is this: it is true and important that actions can be consistent or inconsistent only because they can fulfil descriptions that are consistent or inconsistent. This is the core of truth in the linguistic conception of reason: if practical reason is possible at all, it is possible only because it is possible to reason, think, and therefore talk about what to do. What does not follow from this is that only things that can be said or thought can 'strictly speaking' stand in logical relations, be subject to rational appraisal, and be the sorts of things for which there can be reasons. We have already seen part of the explanation why we draw a conclusion of this sort, namely that it is our talk and thought about things, not the things we talk and think about, that have logical relations, when the things we talk and think about are natural actions and events; e.g., why the actions of natural agents, such as the action of acids on metals, cannot be consistent or inconsistent in this sense, though our talk and thought about them can. But to suppose that such a conclusion can therefore be drawn for human actions is to ignore a vital distinction: the relation between a human action and a description of it can be radically different from the relation between a natural action and a description of it. Both when a person and a natural agent does something, what is done fulfils many descriptions; but some of the descriptions of a human action can be related to that action in a privileged way, for a human action, unlike a natural action, is something that can be done as fulfilling a certain description, the description of the action given in what the agent decides or intends or could decide or intend, or could have decided or intended, to do. In whatever way a particular person's particular decision or intention is identified, it is always ultimately identifiable in terms of what description of action he decides or intends to do; and in doing that thing, if he does it intentionally, he does it *as* an action of that description. In general, since the question of what to do can arise for a human but not for a natural agent, any action description that answers this question will be privileged in this way. Though an action is not something than can be said or put into words, it is something whose relation to what can be put into words, namely the agent's actual or possible decision and intention, enables it to share, as an action of this or that description, some of the logical characteristics of those descriptions. Like thoughts, actions are or can be exercises of mind.

The final point to be made in pursuit of this line of thought is this. The explanation of consistency and inconsistency of actions so far extracted from the 'objection' is incomplete and misleading in an important respect, and completing it will show how the notion of inconsistency in action really is incompatible with the idea that this is to be understood solely in terms of inconsistent beliefs and principles about what should be done. So far the discussion has been about the consistency or inconsistency of one action with another; and under pressure from Hume again, we might suppose that if actions can have logical relations at all, they can have logical relations only with things not 'entirely different' from them, such as other actions. But consistency and inconsistency between actions is possible only because an action (and a decision and intention) can be consistent or inconsistent with things that are not actions (or decisions or intentions): inconsistency between beliefs about what should be done explains inconsistency between things done only if things done (and decisions and intentions) can be consistent or inconsistent with beliefs about what should be done. In general, my breaking a promise (and my decision and intention to break a promise) can be inconsistent with my belief or judgment that I should keep that promise, and with my principle that promises should be kept; if this were not so, no amount of inconsistency between my beliefs or principles would show how my actions could be inconsistent.

4.4. *The generic relation of conformity between action and description*

Of what significance is the occurrence of these notions of consistency and inconsistency in such contexts? Do these words in these contexts really signify 'logical relations' and indicate the possibility of logical appraisal not simply of practical judgments, but of actions themselves? Is not the key notion of the possible inconsistency of an action with a judgment of what should be done indistinguishable, logically speaking, from the notion of an action that disobeys an order? Why should this general idea of conformity or lack of conformity between an action and some description, whether that description occurs in a judgment of what should be done or in an order telling somebody what to do, be thought to carry any implications about the possibility of practical reason? Are not these uses of 'consistent' and 'inconsistent' typical of ordinary language, vague and only vaguely connected with the uses of these words in the logical appraisal of statements and beliefs?

The answer to this last question is that this may be so, but whether it is or not is to be determined only by further enquiry, not by noting that there are differences between the two sorts of consistency and inconsistency and then assuming either that the words are ambiguous or that it is the theoretical kind that is paradigmatically 'logical', or both. Differences in kind may be admitted, but admitting this does not commit us to either of these views. What I shall try to show is that the notions of consistency and inconsistency between action and judgment of action have enough family resemblances to the notions of consistency and inconsistency between judgments or propositions to be accounted members of the same extended family of concepts of reason; and I shall do this by showing how treating these notions in this way enables us to construct a coherent theory of practical reason that solves the problems, clarifies the confusions, and eases the tensions, of the rival theories identified in Chapter 1.

Let us start, then, with the idea of conformity or lack of conformity between an action and some description. By 'a description' I mean what I take Hare to mean by 'a phrastic'—a descriptive noun-phrase, e.g., 'His shutting the door', 'The melting of the ice', 'The book's being heavy', etc., which incorporates the whole content of a possible statement, order, question, or other illocution, omitting only the mood indicator. A negated action description is a possible action description, e.g. 'His not shutting the door', i.e. omissions are possible actions. This does not mean that whenever the statement 'He did not shut the door' is true it answers the question 'What did he do?'. But it does answer this question when he deliberately or intentionally did not shut the door, i.e. when the negation-sign occurs in the description of what he decided or intended, so that we can distinguish between his not deciding or intending to shut the door, and his deciding or intending not to shut the door. In such cases, what he does he does as fulfilling the description 'Not shutting the door'; and we often describe his 'negative action' by saying, e.g., that he refused or forbore to shut the door, or refrained from shutting the door. We may also allow 'He did not shut the door' as an answer to the question 'What did he do?' when it is not the case that he deliberately or intentionally did not shut the door but when he simply failed or omitted to shut the door—the words 'failed' and 'omitted' implying that he should have shut the door.

4.5. *The normative aspect of the logical relation*

This idea of conformity or lack of conformity between an action and some description is an essential part of the idea of consistency or inconsistency between an action and a judgment of action, but not the whole of it. I have already argued that to appraise two items, x and y, as inconsistent is to imply that either x is wrong or unacceptable or *y* is wrong or unacceptable, or both. Actions cannot be true or false and therefore cannot be wrong in the way that beliefs can; but to say that an action is inconsistent with something is to imply that either the action or what it is inconsistent with is wrong, or both. Thus lack of conformity between an action and a description becomes inconsistency only so far as the description itself, or something of which it is a constituent, can be appraised as right or wrong.

Now an action description as such, e.g. 'His shutting the door', is neither right nor wrong, but it can become so by being taken or intended as a description of some action otherwise identified, i.e. by being taken or intended as, or by being a constituent of, a judgment, asserting that that action was, is, or will be done, as when one says, in fact or effect, 'What he did next was: (to) shut the door', or 'His next action was that of shutting the door'. The rightness or wrongness of such descriptions or judgments consists in their being true or false; and since one way of claiming that reports, accounts, predictions, empirical theories, and scientific principles of human conduct (e.g. the principles of classical economics) are false is to say that they are inconsistent with actual behaviour, or with what people in fact do or did, it might seem that the falsity of a descriptive judgment about action is a kind of inconsistency between the judgment and the action it is about. But this would be a mistake. Descriptive judgments about anything, whether actions or not, can be false, reports, accounts, predictions, empirical theories, and scientific principles of anything, whether human conduct, natural actions, the weather, or what not, can be criticised as inconsistent with what actually happens, or with the facts, or with the situation as it really is, or was. But this normal use of 'inconsistent' becomes highly abnormal if we suppose that we have here examples of a general rule connecting falsity and inconsistency, to the effect that a description that is false of *x* is a description that is inconsistent with *x*. Certainly, another way of saying that a description is true or false of *x* is to say that *x* conforms or does not conform to that description, i.e. that *x* is or is not of that description; but to say that *x* does not conform to that description is not to say that it is with *x* that the description is inconsistent. An estate agent's false description of a house may be false by being inconsistent with the facts about the house, but it is not inconsistent with the house itself, or with any of its attributes, such as its size, shape, or number of rooms. When we say, e.g., that the account given in the newspaper was inconsistent with what they actually did (or with the facts, or the facts of their behaviour, etc.) the word 'what' here is again (see 1.6) not the relative 'that which' but the interrogative: what the report is inconsistent with is the fact that, e.g., they tortured the prisoners, where the expression 'they tortured the prisoners' says what they did, i.e. answers the question 'What did they do?'. The alleged inconsistency, therefore, is an inconsistency between the newspaper report and the fact that they tortured the prisoners, not between the report and their torturing the prisoners: for the two things of which one at least is said in this allegation of inconsistency to be wrong or unacceptable are the report and the fact that they tortured the prisoners, not the report and their torturing the prisoners; their torturing the prisoners may be wrong or thought to be wrong, but of such matters this kind of inconsistency is logically independent. Given that the terms of the inconsistency are the report and the fact, the allegation imputes the error to the report by claiming that what it is inconsistent with *is* a fact: inconsistency between the report and what they did implies that the report is wrong because 'what they did' identifies only *correct* answers to the question 'What did they do?'.

When an action description is a constituent of an order, regulation, or rule, we do have a notion of conformity or lack of conformity answering more closely to the notions of consistency and inconsistency. If Smith is ordered to shut the door, it is his not shutting the door that does not conform to (the action description that is a constituent of) the order; and it is this, i.e. his not doing what the order orders or enjoins, that can be said to be inconsistent with the order he was given. Of course, if Smith's action is inconsistent with the order 'Shut the door', addressed to him on a particular occasion, or with the rule or regulation, which on a particular occasion applies to him, e.g. that the last lodger in shuts the door, then it follows that the descriptive statement of fact 'Smith did not on that occasion shut the door' is true. But it is not this statement of fact that is inconsistent with the order, rule or regulation, but Smith's not shutting the door. In his not shutting the door there is nothing that contra*dicts*, that is, there is nothing *said* that is contrary to the order, rule or regulation, but there is something that contra*venes*, that is, there is something *done* that is contrary to, the order, rule, or regulation. A familiar way of describing this situation is to say that Smith disobeyed the order or broke the rule or regulation. To say that Smith's conduct was inconsistent with the order, rule, or regulation is to imply that there was something wrong with either Smith's conduct or the order, rule, or regulation, or both. There are, therefore, two related differences between this kind of case and the case just considered in which, e.g., a newspaper report is said to be inconsistent with what is done. On the one hand, in this kind of case it is somebody's doing something, and not something that is or can be said or stated about what he does, that is one term of the relation; and on the other hand, the other term of the relation, the order, rule, or regulation, is not shown to be wrong simply by a lack of conformity between what is done and its constituent description. These differences essentially distinguish prescriptive from descriptive utterances; naturalism is no less of a fallacy than the anti-naturalistic doctrine of the autonomy of values.

4.6. *The analytic aspect of the logical relation*

I have been concerned with the evaluative aspect of the notion of consistency in conduct, and therefore, so far as the concept of what is logical is involved, with the evaluative aspect of that notion, as it occurs in the distinction between consistency as logical and inconsistency as illogical. But why, we must ask, should this kind of appraisal be regarded as logical in the sense in which that is a term of philosophical classification? Is there any sense in which the relation between action and order is a *logical* rather than a non-logical, say an empirical, relation? Suppose we hear an officer order a subordinate to stand to attention. This is an order on the part of the officer. Now consider something very different from this, namely some action on the part of the subordinate. How do we know what action on the part of the subordinate would conform to that order and what would be contrary to it? We evidently know that his standing to attention would conform to the order, and his not standing to attention would be contrary to it; and we know this simply by understanding the meaning of the order itself, i.e. we know it analytically. The reason for this, of course, is that an order, rule, regulation, practical judgment, or principle of conduct is necessarily something that can be formulated in words containing a description of some action or other, namely of that action that the order, rule, etc., enjoins or prescribes. This is not to say that an order cannot be identified in some other way, as, e.g., the admiral's last order before he sank with his ship; but under this identification the question of what action would conform to that order would be an empirical question depending on the answer to the empirical question 'What was the admiral's last order before he sank with his ship?'. The implication of such a question is that there is necessarily some way of identifying the order referred to other than by the description 'The admiral's last order before he sank with his ship'. The primary way of identifying an order, and a way that must be logically possible, is not by describing it at all, but by formulating or reformulating it, i.e. by putting the order into words and so necessarily describing that action that would conform to it: e.g. 'Take to the boats', or 'Splice the mainbrace'. Given such a formulation, the question what action would conform to it has an answer that is not empirical but analytic: the answer is, an action of that description occurring in the order.[1]

In 1.6 I quoted Kant's reference to 'the deduction of actions from principles'. Shall we say that the relation in question is deductive? Well, it is certainly not inductive, and if we had to choose between these two the characterisation 'deductive' would be the less misleading. But a deduction or induction is a kind of argument or inference, and to distinguish logical relations in terms of their being deductive, inductive, and so on, would be to draw a distinction within the field of those relations that hold between the relevant elements of an argument or inference, i.e. propositions, facts, premises, and conclusions. Since taking to the boats or splicing the mainbrace cannot be inferred or drawn as a conclusion they cannot, we had better say, be related deductively (or inductively) to the admiral's order. The word 'analytic', embracing as it does the area of deductive relations, locates the relation in question on the right side of the deductive–inductive divide, and being more of a term of art, its meaning less entangled with the concepts of argument and inference, is more appropriate.

It may perhaps be objected that what is really analytic here is the relation between two statements, namely 'The admiral ordered them to take to the boats' and 'Their taking to the boats would

---

[1] Some versions of rule or indirect utilitarianism say that particular actions are justified by their conformity to a rule that is justified by its utility, i.e. by its effects, including particular actions. Some of the troubles of this doctrine are traceable to the tendency to run together this essential characteristic of rules, that they specify analytically what actions *conform* to them, with the empirical notion of actions as *effects* of rules.

conform (or would have conformed) to the admiral's order'. But this would be like denying that there is an analytic relation between the two statements 'It's a triangle' and 'It's three-sided' and claiming rather that what is analytic is the relation between '*A* said that it's a triangle' and 'That it's three-sided followed from what *A* said'. These are not exclusive alternatives: the last pair of statements is analytically related because the relation of following from referred to in the second of this pair is itself (in this context) an analytic relation. My contention is that an analogous point holds for the first pair of statements. Because it holds in virtue of the meaning of the words identifying its two terms, the relation in which doing something stands to an order, rule, or judgment that something be done, when it conforms or is contrary to such an order, rule, or judgment, is an analytic relation; and it is the analyticity of this relation, embedded in the evaluative notion of the consistency or inconsistency of an action with an order, rule, or judgment, that enables these terms 'consistent' and 'inconsistent' to continue to function, even in these practical contexts, as terms of *logical* appraisal.

4.7. *The possibility of doing what is inconsistent with one's practical judgments*

Now if I think that there will be a slump and you think that there will not be a slump, what I think is inconsistent with what you think; this inconsistency is between what you think and what I think, not between my thinking this and your thinking that, nor in my thinking or in your thinking. One of us must be wrong in thinking what we do, but neither of us is thereby inconsistent. When two propositions are inconsistent, believing those propositions is inconsistent only when this believing is the believing of one and the same person at one and the same time: the formulation of the normative implication B6 (3.1) is 'It is inconsistent to think that *p* and at the same time think that *q*', and the infinitive form of the verb 'to think', occurring without a subject, indicates that the thinking in question, for it to be inconsistent, must be the thinking of one and the same person. Similar considerations apply to the notion of consistency in practical contexts. If a student's conduct is inconsistent with the regulations, the inconsistency is attributable neither to the student and his conduct nor to the regulations. But it is possible for a person's conduct to be contrary to his own rules, principles, or judgments, i.e. in general to his own beliefs about what he should do, beliefs that he has even at that moment when he does what is contrary to them; and so we can say such things as 'His conduct was inconsistent with his own principles, convictions, judgment, view, belief about the right thing to do' and (parallel to B6) 'It is inconsistent to think that one should do x and at the same time do y' where 'doing x' and 'doing y' are incompatible action descriptions. To say that these action descriptions are incompatible is to say that it is logically impossible for anyone to do both x and y on one and the same occasion, i.e. that 'A did x and at the same time did y' is necessarily false because self-contradictory. But to say that it is inconsistent to think that one should do x and at the same time do y is not to say that thinking this and at the same time doing that is logically impossible, but rather that it is logically impermissible, i.e. that 'A thought that he should do x but did y' is necessarily not self-contradictory, but states something that is logically possible. When we say that it is possible for someone's actions to be inconsistent with his principles of conduct, we are using the word 'inconsistent' as a term of logical appraisal, i.e. in the sense that it has in List B; and the relevant contrasts implied between what is logically possible and what is not run parallel to those for theoretical contexts outlined in 3.14.

In 1.5 I described a dilemma resulting from Hare's attempt to combine an account of practical reason with a linguistic conception of reason. Typically, such an attempt identifies practical reason with practical inference; and if we say, in accordance with the linguistic conception, that actions cannot have logical relations with anything, or be inferred, or be conclusions from premises, the concession involved in allowing the possibility of practical inference, in which arguments can have such 'practical' conclusions as imperatives, seems to leave actions themselves still outside the scope of reason. The question that this raises is: in what sense are practical inferences practical, i.e. how exactly are the conclusions of practical arguments related to action? As we saw, Hare's answer rejects the view that the relation is either purely contingent or essentially causal and therefore empirical, and claims that it is, rather, a logical relation: value-judgments in general, including what I have been calling practical judgments, e.g. that one ought to shut the door, entail self-addressed imperatives, e.g. 'Shut the door', and assenting to the imperative, and therefore to the value-judgment, necessarily involves, when the occasion arises and it is in one's power, doing what the imperative enjoins, e.g. shutting the door. In 1.5 I suggested that this account seemed to imply not that actions could be inferences from value-judgments but only that statements about actions could be inferences from statements about value-judgments. In fact, the merit of Hare's view is that it avoids the first of these ideas, which I have argued should be rejected, without implying that the second constitutes all that can be said on the relation of reason to action. Hare's account implies that though actions cannot be conclusions of arguments, i.e. they cannot be *what* one infers, nevertheless assenting to a practical judgment, and therefore inferring such a judgment, involves, when the occasion arises, performing the appropriate action. In practical inference, what one infers is, e.g., that one should shut the door; shutting the door is not what one infers but is what is involved in inferring that one should shut the door. By implication, then, Hare at this point resists the temptation to contrast practical with theoretical reason by contrasting a conception of practice as things that can be done with a conception of theory as things that can be said, and instead compares and contrasts doing things with assenting to (and therefore inferring) things that can be said. The door now stands open for the step explained in Chapter 3: the step of acknowledging that logical relations between things that can be said bear normatively on assenting to (and therefore inferring) those things. Hare does not take the step, his way presumably barred by the doctrine of the naturalistic fallacy, i.e. in his version the doctrine that no prescriptive conclusions follow from premises that are not prescriptive; accordingly, as he sees, on his account of the logical relation between practical judgment and action, strictly interpreted, 'it becomes analytic to say that everyone always does what he thinks he ought to . . .',[1] i.e. it becomes logically impossible for anyone, when the occasion arises and he is able to do it, not to do what he thinks he ought to, and there can be no such thing as *akrasia*, weakness of will. The step that Hare does not take, however, makes available, as an alternative to intuitionism's contingent conception, to the causal theory of Hume and Stevenson, and to his own logical account, the view of the relation between practical judgments and action that I have outlined: the relation is neither purely contingent, nor causal, nor logical in Hare's sense, but normatively logical. Not the least (philosophical)

[1] op. cit., p. 169.

advantage of such a view over Hare's is that it makes it logically possible, without recourse to the elaborate manœuvres in his *Freedom and Reason*,[1] for people not to do what they think they ought to: there is no logical impossibility in being inconsistent, either in belief or in action.

In 3.16 and 3.17 I allowed that the notions of consistency and inconsistency between propositions do not have normative implications in some cases: in those cases, namely, when recognising that two propositions are inconsistent is a necessary condition of understanding their meaning in that minimal sense that is itself a necessary condition of believing (or disbelieving) them; in such cases, I said, it is impossible to think, inconsistently, both that p and that q, because the statement 'A thinks both that p and that q' is itself inconsistent. How is it that 'A thinks that he ought to do x but does not do x' is not similarly inconsistent? How is it that doing x is not a necessary condition of understanding the meaning of the statement that one ought to do x, and therefore of believing that one ought to do x? Put like this, the suggestion seems ludicrous. *My* doing x is not a necessary condition of understanding the statement that *he* ought to do x, and there seems nothing more to understanding the statement that I ought to do x except what is involved in understanding the differences in use between the pronouns 'he' and 'I'. What is necessary to understanding the meaning of 'One ought to do x' is recognising that it is inconsistent both to believe this and, if and when the occasion arises, not do x, meaning not to do it: it is this that has its analogue in the theoretical case. The difference is that in central cases of belief it is logically possible to believe what is inconsistent only if it is not known or believed to be inconsistent: i.e. it is possible both for someone to believe that p and that q and for the propositions that p and that q to be inconsistent, but not for someone to believe that p and that q believing or knowing the propositions that p and that q to be inconsistent. For to believe or know that 'p' is inconsistent with 'q' is to believe or know that one of them at least is false, and it is logically impossible for anyone to think or know that what he thinks is false. This is why, in the central cases of belief, the kind of wrongness involved in being inconsistent must be the kind involved in being *mistaken*. To mistake something is to take or think it to be otherwise than as it is, and so to be wrong not thinking or knowing that one is wrong. Now it is, of course,

[1] Oxford, 1965, ch. 5.

possible to be mistaken in action, i.e. to do something mistakenly
or by mistake: this is the same notion of mistake, since to do
something by mistake is to do it taking or thinking it to be otherwise than as it is. But unlike the 'theoretical' case, it is also
possible both for someone to believe that he ought to do something on a certain occasion and to do something on that occasion
which he thinks or knows to be inconsistent with that belief. This
is not thereby to do that thing *by mistake*, since he must in such a
case think or know that he is wrong. But there are ways of being
wrong in action other than by being mistaken; and so the general
notion of something's being contrary to reason includes the
paradigm theoretical case of being mistaken, but can also, as far
as action is concerned, take other forms, from being weak-willed
at one extreme to deliberately, perhaps with a strength of will like
Satan's in *Paradise Lost*, flouting reason at the other. These other
possible ways of being wrong are essential to the nature of action
and constitute one of the essential differences between action and
belief: without them there could be no concept of the will.

4.8. *How there can be reasons for doing things, though*
actions cannot be conclusions of arguments

We are now in a position to see why it is tempting to think of
actions as possible conclusions of arguments, though wrong, and
how nevertheless actions are the sorts of things that there can be
reasons for or against. The demonstration consists in exhibiting
the general conceptual analogies and disanalogies, connections
and disconnections, between the notion of a reason for thinking
something and the notion of a reason for doing something. Let us
first rehearse schematically the conceptual situation in the
theoretical field. Suppose we have: the proposition that q follows
from the proposition that p. Then we can also have: the argument
'p, so q'; the inference 'from the fact that p, I infer that q'; and the
giving of a reason 'The fact that p is a (conclusive) reason for
thinking that q'. Consider now an item *not-r*, which is inconsistent
with the judgment that q. Our question is: given that *not-r* has this
relation to the proposition that q, what relations can it consequently stand in to the proposition that p? If '*not-r*' expresses a
proposition we can have: the proposition that r follows from the
proposition that p; the argument 'p, so r'; the inference 'From the
fact that p I infer that r'; and (under certain restrictions that need
not for the moment concern us) the giving of a reason 'The fact

that *p* is a (conclusive) reason for thinking that *r*'. If, however, '*not-r*' is an action description, there will be no analogues to the first three of these, but the fourth will turn out to be 'The fact that *p* is a (conclusive) reason for doing *r*'. In this case, of course, the judgment that *q* will be the practical judgment that *r* ought to be done. *Prima facie*, at any rate, such judgments, unlike actions, can be inferred, drawn as conclusions in arguments; and because actions, though incapable of being inferred, can be consistent or inconsistent with such judgments, a premise from which such a judgment can be inferred, and which is therefore a reason for thinking that *r* ought to be done, is necessarily also a reason for doing *r*. In figurative terms: the pressure of reason exerted by the premises on a practical conclusion is transmitted, through the logical relation in which an action can stand to such a conclusion, to the action itself. The relation is symmetrical, and no valves restrict the transmission of pressure to one direction: a reason for doing something is also a reason for thinking that it ought to be done.

This does not, of course, show that there is such a thing as practical reason. What it does is to show how it is possible for reason to be practical, despite certain arguments to the contrary. More specifically, it shows that the distinction between theory and practice, drawn as the distinction between propositions and actions or more liberally between what can be said and what can be done, can seem to lead to the sceptical conclusion only through a misconception of the nature of reason. In particular, the insights in Hume's argument to this sceptical conclusion can, in the light of what I have said, be turned against that conclusion.

Hume's argument depends on this principle, that practical judgments are practical, i.e. related to action, in such a way that if such judgments could be inferred, drawn as conclusions of arguments, so also could actions. Since actions cannot be inferred, cannot be conclusions of arguments, it would follow that practical judgments cannot be either. Practical judgments, therefore, could not strictly be judgments, propositions, true or false: they must be, say, expressions of emotion or sentiment, and morality 'is more properly felt that judg'd of'.[1]

There is no denying that practical judgments and morality have much to do with actions, feelings, and emotions. The conclusion that sticks in the gullet, as clean contrary to the relevant conceptual facts, is the conclusion that we cannot assert, deny, state,

[1] op. cit., p. 470.

believe, infer, or doubt that, e.g., one ought not to practise racial discrimination. Its contrariety to the conceptual facts might be defended; but not in Hume's manner. In my reconstruction of his argument the conclusion is drawn from premises that seem conceptually conformist, such as that actions cannot be inferred from propositions. The oddity is that this conformist premise should yield the non-conformist conclusion that there therefore cannot, strictly speaking, be reasons for or against doing things. The remedy lies in the distinction, though not disconnection, between the notion of reasons for and against things and those of inference and argument, and so in correcting the principle on which Hume's argument rests: practical judgments are practical, i.e. related to action, in such a way that if such judgments could follow from others and thus be inferred, drawn as conclusions of arguments, it would follow not that actions could be inferred, drawn as conclusions of arguments, but rather that the premises of those arguments, in being reasons for accepting those judgments, would necessarily also be reasons for acting consistently with those judgments. This principle puts practice into its right relation to theory in the family of concepts of reason: the notions of doing something and believing something, members of the nuclear group of psychological concepts, are connected through the normative notion of a reason for something, and this normative notion in its turn connects with the nuclear group of logical relation concepts, such as those of following from and consistency. The key concepts of following from, inference, reason, thinking, and doing, enter into the principle in accordance with the following three conceptual truths: if from the fact that p it follows that q, then from the fact that p one can infer that q; if from the fact that p one can infer that q, the fact that p is a (conclusive) reason for thinking that q; and if the proposition that q is a practical proposition, e.g. that one ought to do x, then a reason for thinking that q is a reason for doing x. The connection stated in this last truth, between a reason for thinking something and a reason for doing something, is the connection mediated by the possibility of an action's being consistent or inconsistent with a practical judgment.

It is worth noticing that there is no incompatibility between what was said in Chapter 3 about the moral appraisal of belief and action and my claim that a reason for doing something is necessarily a reason for believing something; and in particular,

3.25–3.27 have no tendency, in conjunction with the argument of this present section, to show that practical judgments are not strictly judgments and cannot strictly be *believed*. If a reason for doing something is a moral reason, that consideration bears morally on, i.e. on the morality of, doing that thing; but in being also a reason, and if you wish a moral reason, for believing something, namely that that thing should, ought to, or must be done, it does not as such bear morally on, i.e. on the morality of, believing that thing. Its bearing on believing that thing is of course normative, but the related normative notions of rightly and wrongly believing that thing are those essentially connected with the notion of belief, and therefore with the notion of truth, as explained in 3.21 and 3.22.

Hume's argument, and the pressures underlying it, can now be seen for what they are worth. In pondering the possibility of practical reason we are faced with three considerations not easy to reconcile: practical judgments can be believed, disbelieved, doubted, asserted, denied, and inferred, and can therefore occur as conclusions of arguments; actions cannot; but the sense in which practical judgments are practical, i.e. related to action, requires that in the question of practical *reason* what goes for judgments goes also for actions. Aristotle in effect denies the second consideration. Intuitionism (or ethical rationalism) typically solves the problem by denying the last consideration and so representing practical judgments as theoretical, unrelated to action in this respect. Hume, to his credit, realises that the third consideration must be preserved, and that this constitutes a decisive objection to intuitionism:[1] taking his stand firmly on the second and third considerations, he solves the problem by rejecting the first. The principle I have formulated in correction of Hume's shows that none of these three considerations needs to be rejected. That they appear to be incompatible is the effect of a certain conception of the nature of reason, a conception in which the notion of reason in the last consideration is identified with the notion of inference or argument in the first and second, i.e. in which practical reason is identified with practical inference or argument. If this conception of reason is now added as a fourth consideration to the three above, it might be thought that there is nothing to choose between Hume's course of rejecting the first and

[1] Contrary to Blanshard's account of Hume: see my critical notice of his *Reason and Goodness* in *Mind,* October 1966, esp. pp. 594–5.

my course of rejecting the fourth. My claim is that rejecting the
fourth, i.e. recognising that inference and argument are not the
only exercises of reason, is more consistent with the meaning of
the word 'reason', and is in any case involved, as Chapter 3
shows, in the notions of inference and argument themselves.

4.9. *Imperatives and practical judgments as answers to questions of what to do*

The two connected analytic relations I have drawn attention to
between actions and practical judgments, between doing and
thinking that something is the case, i.e. the possible consistency or
inconsistency between an action and a judgment, and the necessary
connection between a reason for thinking that one ought to do
something and a reason for doing that thing, constitute the basis
of an account of the sense in which practical judgments and beliefs
are practical and in particular of how they can be practical
without ceasing to be judgments or beliefs. Now it will be noticed
that though I began to elucidate the former relation, of consistency and inconsistency, in terms not only of practical judgments
but also of orders, rules, regulations and so on, my account of the
latter relation, involving the notion of a reason for doing something, has been conducted in terms of practical judgments to the
exclusion of orders, rules, and regulations. This needs explaining.
The explanation will show how, though these items share enough
of the essential features of practical judgments to make it plausible
to give an account of practical reason in terms of them, their
possession of other features raises irrelevant problems.

Giving somebody an order is an illocutionary act that typically
involves an utterance in the imperative mood, e.g. 'Hang it there',
'Don't delay', 'Send for reinforcements'. But the imperative mood
has many uses, and in different circumstances many different
illocutionary acts could be performed by uttering the same
imperative sentences, e.g. advising, inviting, warning, suggesting,
instructing, laying down a rule or regulation, and so on. Some of
these at least, e.g. advising, suggesting, and instructing, are
illocutionary acts in which one person tries to answer another's
question of what to do; and the same imperative as is used by one
person in advising another what to do may be regarded as
answering the second's question of what to do even when that
answer is his own answer—he may, that is, be regarded as
uttering a self-addressed imperative in answer to that question.

Brown[1] has explained why imperatives are logically so well suited to this role.

A question of what to do is a question answered by anything that says what to do, i.e. by any utterance identifying something as the (or a) thing to do. The imperative 'Hang it there' answers the question of what to do by saying in effect that the thing to do is: hang it there. It is only as an answer to someone's question of what to do that the analogy with practical judgment can be pressed. Any question that makes sense has a sense that determines a range of intelligible answers to it, and it must in principle be possible for some of these answers to be better than others, i.e. more, or more nearly, correct, and perhaps for one of them to be right and the others wrong. Thus with respect to the question of what to do we can wonder what to do, consider what to do, and think about what to do; and the successful outcome of these things is that we then know what to do, or at least think correctly that the thing to do is, e.g., hang it there. Precisely this condition, as I have pointed out, is necessary if an imperative is to be consistent or inconsistent with anything, such as an action: for if two things are inconsistent, one at least must be wrong or in error, and for an imperative and an action to be inconsistent it must be possible for either or both to be wrong.

What then is it for an imperative to be wrong or in error as an answer to the question of what to do? It seems clearly to be this, that since, as an answer to that question, the imperative 'Hang it there' says in effect that the thing to do is hang it there, this imperative would be wrong if that were the wrong thing to do, or at least if it were not the right thing to do, i.e. if that were not the thing that the person whose question it is ought to do. It follows that as an answer to the question of what to do the imperative 'Hang it there' is indistinguishable from the practical judgment 'I (you, he) ought to hang it there'. For in accordance with the logic of belief outlined in 3.22, which, as I have said, holds equally for practical judgments, the judgment that he ought to hang it there would be wrong or in error if and only if hanging it there were not the thing he ought to do. Thus the question whether the imperative were right or wrong, correct or incorrect, would be indistinguishable from the question whether the corresponding practical judgment were right or wrong, correct or incorrect. The judgment and imperative would be 'transparent' answers to the

[1] op. cit., 1.10.

question in the way in which believing is transparent: the right answer to somebody's question of what to do would be that answer specifying the right thing for him to do; and any reason favouring that answer would be a reason favouring the doing of that thing. As an answer to the question of what to do, therefore, an imperative is implicitly, if not explicitly, evaluative or normative.

The artificiality of what I have just said is a consequence of isolating an imperative common to many different illocutionary acts, i.e. of treating a whole range of different illocutionary acts as typically involving the utterance of an imperative, and then considering what it would be for such an imperative to be a correct answer to somebody's question of what to do. Now to talk of something's being an answer to a question is already to classify it in terms of an illocutionary act, namely the act of answering a question, i.e. the act of giving an answer to a question by saying some such thing as 'Hang it there'. We could say, vaguely enough, that the notion of an answer to a question is an abstraction from the notion of answering a question, an abstraction achieved by defining the former notion in terms of the transparency of the latter. Closely connected as these two notions are, they can be distinguished in various ways, and in particular in a way relevant to our problem: the correct, right, or best answer to a question is not necessarily the answer that it would be correct, right, or best to give on any particular occasion.[1] Answering a question is itself doing something, and the further question of whether to do this thing, and what thing of this general sort to do, e.g. what answer to give, may arise for someone for whom the original question arises. In this way any question, say whether it rained last night, or whether to hang it there, generates an infinite progeny of further questions, questions of the form: 'whether, and if so, how, to answer the question whether . . .'. In general, of course, we treat the question of what answer to give to the question whether p as indistinguishable from the question whether p, and if we did not at some point in the succession of generated questions insist on this identity no question could ever be answered. Some concepts connected with the notions of question and answer, as the concept of thinking is, are such that this indistinguishability is logically necessary: somebody's thinking can be identified by the question thought about and his settlement of (answer to) that

[1] See my objection to Hare, 2.3.

question, as when somebody thinks about or wonders whether it rained last night and so comes to think that it rained last night; and as I have already argued, somebody's question of whether to think that it rained last night is for him indistinguishable from the question whether it rained last night. Now when someone is thinking or wondering whether to do x, and so comes to think that the thing to do is x, the same transparency holds (and indeed, thinking that the thing to do is x is one form of thinking that p). If, therefore, for the purpose of analysis, we treat this thinking as a kind of saying to oneself and so regard this situation as one in which someone asks (himself) what to do and answers (himself) with a self-addressed imperative 'Do x', i.e. if that imperative answer is given by that same person whose question of what to do it answers, this notion of answering that question will also be transparent. No one can distinguish his own question of what to do from his own question of what answer to give to that question. Except in its role of identifying the locution involved, the illocutionary act in this situation, being transparent, will disappear from the analysis.

But in general, though answering the question whether to hang it there may be regarded as common to all illocutionary acts in which someone utters the imperative 'Hang it there', the transparency of this imperative as an answer to that question is not fully preserved in the notion of the illocutionary act of answering the question. Typically, this is an act in which one person answers another's question of what to do. Considerations other than whether the thing to do is hang it there will enter into the question whether to answer 'Hang it there'; and in this way the original simplicity of the question will give way to complexity. Between his question of whether to hang it there and my question of whether to answer 'Hang it there', there will be a material distinction; and a reason I may have for answering 'Hang it there' will not necessarily be a reason that he has for hanging it there. This is even more obviously the case when this genus of illocutions, answering somebody's question of what to do, is divided into its species, such as advising somebody to do something, instructing him to do something, or suggesting that he do something; for the differences between these more specific concepts reflect differences in the situations to which they are appropriate, differences that may have a bearing on my question of what to do when you ask me what to do. The best answer to your question might be 'Hang it there', but the best answer to my question could be 'Advise him to hang it there' or 'Instruct him to hang it there' or 'Suggest to him that he hang it there' or even, if you are counter-suggestible, 'Suggest to him that he hang it elsewhere'. In the first three cases, the words I utter could be indistinguishable from the words that constitute your answer to your question, though the question whether I was in a position, in uttering these words, thereby to instruct you, or only, say, to advise you, would be a material consideration in my question of what to do. To regard the illocutionary act of answering somebody's question of what to do as the genus of these more specific illocutions is already to stretch the concept of that act, but to stretch it still further to include such things as inviting somebody to do something, or warning somebody not to do something, or giving orders, or laying down rules or regulations for somebody to follow, brings in even more contextual considerations to complicate the original simplicity of the relation between the question of what to do and the right answer to that question.[1] That simplicity is preserved if we confine ourselves to practical judgments as the range of items that answer the question. As a judgment, e.g. that he should hang it there, such an item can occur not only in the context of an illocutionary act but also, unlike an imperative, as something believed or disbelieved; and this context guarantees its transparency as an answer to the question. A reason that Smith has for hanging it there is a reason that in principle anybody has, regardless of his situation, for thinking that Smith should hang it there; for it is simply a reason for thinking that Smith should hang it there, without restriction to the thinking of any particular person and his circumstances, especially his relation to Smith.

Thus, though the imperative 'Hang it there' and the judgment 'You ought to hang it there' are both in a form adapted to the

[1] This complication is one source of indirect utilitarianism. To the question 'What ought we to do?' hedonistic utilitarianism replies with the universal imperative 'Promote happiness'. This rule or principle or criterion formulated or laid down by utilitarianism is transparent: the question 'What rule, principle, or criterion of conduct should we have?' is treated, naturally enough, as indistinguishable from the question 'What should we do?'; for the answer to this latter question, namely 'Promote happiness', is itself a rule, principle, or criterion. This is, of course, compatible with the claim that the notion of a rule, principle, or criterion can occur in some conceptual contexts that are not transparent: with the claim, e.g., that the question 'What rules should we apply or use in settling the question of what to do?' can be distinguished from the question of what to do.

answering of a question of what to do, namely of the question arising for that person to whom they are addressed, the fact that the latter expresses something that can be thought or believed marks an important distinction. But how sharply can this distinction be drawn? Is there not some sense in which the imperative too expresses something that can be thought? Since one of the distinctions between imperatives and practical judgments is that the former are always addressed to somebody, imperatives, unlike practical judgments, typically have no subject: the person whose action is in question is in these cases the person to whom the imperative is addressed. In some circumstances (e.g. when more than two people are present and there may be some doubt about whose action is in question) the person to whom the imperative is addressed may be explicitly identified, e.g. 'Smith, hang it there'. It would be wrong to say that the name 'Smith' here functions as the subject of the imperative sentence: it simply serves to identify the person to whom that sentence is addressed, and it may occur in an identical role in introducing an indicative sentence whose subject is other than the person addressed, e.g. 'Smith, arsenic is a poison'. However, someone different from the person addressed may be ordered to do something, as in the sentence, 'Smith will hang it there'; and we may allow this as an imperative with a subject. It is the nearest thing to a third-person counterpart of an expression of intention 'I will hang it there'; and indeed, if one person intends another to do something, an imperative, particularly when used as an order, in whatever person, typically expresses that intention. Someone who says and means, in this sense, 'Smith will hang it there', intends Smith to hang it there. We have already seen that someone who intends to do something thinks that he will do that thing. Is it the case that if Jones intends Smith to hang it there it follows that Jones thinks that Smith will hang it there? Is it the case, in other words, that if Jones orders Smith to hang it there by saying 'Smith will hang it there' Jones thereby expresses the thought that Smith will hang it there? Can an imperative be regarded as expressing the content of a thought? Would his saying 'Smith will hang it there but I don't think that he will' involve the same sort of inconsistency as his saying 'It will rain tomorrow but I don't think that it will'? Whatever the answers to these questions, we face two alternatives. If an imperative is held to express a thought that is indistinguishable from the intention, it will not be the kind of thought that is inferable, but the kind identified in 1.6.

If on the other hand it is inferable, its relation to the action it refers to will be theoretical, not practical, i.e. it will be simply a prediction, not an intention. Either way it differs radically from the corresponding practical judgment.

Thus imperatives, like practical judgments, can have subjects, including subjects other than the person(s) to whom they are addressed; and they in some circumstances essentially express a persisting state of mind in certain ways similar to belief, namely intending somebody to do something. Two important differences remain, connected with the one noted at the end of the preceding paragraph. First, one person can intend another to do something only if he occupies some fairly specific relationship to him, i.e., roughly, only if he is in a position to give him orders or tell him what to do. Second, though it is possible for someone to have intended somebody to do something in the past, imperatives have no past tense and it is impossible for someone in the present to intend somebody to have done something in the past. Practical judgments are limited in neither way. The formula 'A thinks that B ought to x' implies no restrictions on the range of the variables A and B, except that they range over people (or rational beings), and no restriction of past, present, or future on the range of the act variable x; provided only that the question of whether to do the thing arose, arises, or will arise for the agent himself, so that he could intend or could have intended to do it, anybody's action, at whatever time, is in principle available to anybody as a subject for a practical judgment. The identity of a practical judgment, therefore, is independent of its temporal relation to its subject, and independent of any relation between the person making the judgment and the person whose action is the subject of that judgment. If I now think that Smith ought to hang it there tomorrow, and you think the day after tomorrow that Smith ought to have hung it there yesterday, you and I make the same judgment; and if I am right in thinking it, you are right too. In this respect also practical judgments really are judgments, and share with empirical judgments the common 'cognitive' possibilities of being believed, disbelieved, doubted, etc.

4.10. *The meaning of the word 'ought'*

I have so far identified what I have called practical judgments only vaguely, as judgments in which it is said of someone that he should, must, or ought to do something; and I have suggested not only that their being judgments but also that their being practical is due to their containing such a word as 'should', 'ought', or 'must', which enables them to be judgments that are rationally related to action, i.e. related to action in such a way that actions can be consistent or inconsistent with them, and in such a way that a reason for doing something is a reason for thinking that that thing should, must, or ought to be done. In formulating this sense of their being practical, however, I have relied heavily on the fact that the context of the discussion has naturally tended to impose such a practical interpretation on judgments identified in the above vague way. The fact is that judgments of that form are not necessarily practical. The word 'must', expressing necessity, clearly occurs in judgments that are of that form but which are not practical in the sense defined. 'Smith must hang it there' is ambiguous between a practical and a theoretical interpretation: in the practical interpretation it is an answer to Smith's question of what to do, and says in effect that necessarily the thing for Smith to do is hang it there; in the theoretical interpretation it is a prediction, an answer to the question of what Smith will in fact do, and it says in effect that necessarily the thing that Smith will do is hang it there. In the theoretical interpretation of the judgment the role of the word 'must' is of the same general kind as in any other prediction in which it is said that something must happen, e.g. 'The leaves must turn brown before they drop off'. In the past tense the distinction is clearly marked by a grammatical difference: the practical judgment becomes 'Smith had to hang it there' and the theoretical 'Smith must have hung it there'.

It has been less commonly recognised that the words 'should' and 'ought' show the same flexibility, and are equally indifferent as between practical and theoretical judgments. The importance of the word 'ought' in moral judgments has misled some philosophers into thinking of it as a peculiarly moral word. Other philosophers, noticing its occurrence in prudential judgments such as 'You ought to see the dentist about your tooth-ache', have corrected this mistake and have claimed that its peculiar function is to make a judgment not specifically moral but generally practical. But this also is to be misled. Its role is still wider. Like the judgment with 'must', 'Smith ought to hang it there' is ambiguous between a practical and a theoretical interpretation, and in the theoretical interpretation the word 'ought' functions in the same general way as in any other prediction in which it is said that something ought to happen, e.g. 'The leaves ought to turn brown before they drop off'; or, to give an example that even philosophers estranged from its ordinary meaning ought to remember as not entirely unfamiliar, 'On all the evidence, it ought to be a fine day tomorrow'.

If the words 'must' and 'can', expressing necessity and possibility, are classed as modal words, the word 'ought' is also a modal word. If the word 'ought' is a normative word, so also are the words 'must' and 'can'. They belong to the same family, though specialist philosophical preoccupations, on the one hand with formal logic, and therefore with so-called logical (i.e. analytic) necessity and possibility, and on the other hand with ethics, and therefore with the concept expressed by the word 'ought', have tended to obscure this conceptual fact.[1] Recognition that matters of logic are themselves, explicitly or by implication, evaluative or normative opens the way to recognising the concepts expressed by the words 'ought', 'must', 'should', and 'can' as belonging to this general class of logically normative concepts: in the words of Brown's conjecture,[2] 'modal concepts in general express the pressure of reason for or against doing things which people do' (in a wide sense of 'do'). All necessity, we may say, is logical necessity—as long as the word 'logical' here refers not simply to what is analytic but to reason in all its exercises. The word 'must' expresses that pressure in which there is conclusive reason for someone to do something (including the case in which 'do' is a stand-in for 'think' or 'believe'); the word 'ought' that pressure in which there is good (but not necessarily conclusive) reason to do something; and so on. The emotivist doctrine that practical judgments are essentially non-rational is a more than usually stark perversion of the truth.

One of the chief problems raised by this idea is how on this theory to explain the conspicuous asymmetry between the occurrence of these modal words in practical contexts and their occurrence in theoretical contexts. Since in the practical case any reason is a reason for doing something and in the theoretical case any reason is a reason for thinking something, we might expect a distribution of modal words that is symmetrical between the two

[1] Though not from Kant, whose overriding interest in the scope of reason, in practice as well as theory, gave him a vantage point from which this truth could be clearly seen.
[2] op. cit., 3.9.

cases: that there is good reason for Smith to hang it there we express by saying that Smith ought to hang it there; and symmetrically, that there is good reason for thinking that Smith will hang it there would be expressed by saying that we ought to think that Smith will hang it there. The word 'ought' would then connect directly with the verb denoting that item for which there is good reason—Smith's action in the practical case, anybody's thinking in the theoretical case. As I have pointed out, we can discern plenty of parallels between the appraisal of action and the appraisal of belief, parallels to some extent reflected in grammatical and syntactical similarities in the occurrence of words of appraisal and their association with the appropriate theoretical and practical verbs or verbal nouns. But the expectation of symmetry in the occurrence of the modal words between these two contexts is disappointed when we find that the typical case for theoretical contexts is not the one given above, i.e. that we ought to think that Smith will hang it there, but rather, simply, as in the practical case, that Smith ought to hang it there; so that this locution, as I have pointed out, becomes ambiguous between a practical and a theoretical interpretation. How is it that the modal word gets displaced, so to speak, from its association with the verb 'think' to association with the verb denoting that action or happening that the thinking is about? It was Hume's merit to have recognised that such a displacement occurs with the concept of causal necessity, but his account of it is too open to sceptical interpretations to make it acceptable. I have nothing of substance to add to Brown's elegant explanation.[1] In my terms, the displacement occurs because of the transparency of belief. The practical question in my example is Smith's question of whether to hang it there. The theoretical question whose formulation bears the closest grammatical analogy to this is the question of whether to think that Smith will hang it there; and this formulation, analogously with the practical one, introduces explicitly into the question that item for or against which any consideration will count as a reason, namely, thinking something. But this question is indistinguishable from one that is not a normative question about thinking something but a factual question in which the notion of thinking does not occur, the question whether Smith will hang it there. Since the answer to this question need contain no reference to anybody's thinking anything, the modal word expressing the

[1] op. cit., 3.3.

pressure of reason favouring that answer will be grammatically associated with those words describing Smith's (expected) action, e.g. 'Smith ought to hang it there'. It is this displacement, in which the modal qualification is attached to that item which the thinking is about rather than to what is under the pressure of reason, the thinking itself, that tends to conceal the normative nature of modal concepts in theoretical contexts.

To the extent that types of reasons, considerations, and therefore arguments, can be distinguished we can also distinguish types of necessity, possibility, and so on. The context usually makes clear the type involved, and so makes it superfluous to identify that type explicitly, e.g. as 'logical' (analytic) possibility, or moral, legal, or causal necessity. But by widening or narrowing the field of considerations we may change the modality of an item: what it may be empirically impossible for a man to do may be possible from an analytic point of view, i.e. taking into account a different range of considerations. Many philosophical problems hinge on the relations between these different types of considerations, and therefore between the different kinds of modal qualifications that can attach to one and the same item. We know that 'must' implies 'can'; we know too that 'ought' implies 'can': but when such implications cross from one field of consideration into another, as when 'He morally must or ought to do that' implies 'He empirically can do that', there we have a problem.

This view of modal concepts, and in particular their displacement in theoretical contexts, throws light on a number of dark issues. First, it helps to disentangle some of the complications noticed in the notions of 'logical' possibility and impossibility in 3.14. If the proposition that p is inconsistent with the proposition that q, then it is logically impossible, as we say, both that p and that q. It is not upon the situation 'described' by this inconsistent conjunction that the modal concept bears normatively, but upon thinking both that p and that q. It is a mistake to suppose, therefore, that the modal concept qualifies that thinking in the same way that it qualifies what that thinking is about; except, of course, in the limiting cases in which not only 'p and q', but also 'A thinks that p and that q', is inconsistent.

Second, in this account of modal concepts we also have an explanation of the logical relations I have outlined between actions and practical judgments. Since the practical judgment that Smith ought to, should, or must hang it there expresses the pressure of reason in favour of Smith's hanging it there, any fact that is a reason for Smith to hang it there will also be a reason for thinking that he ought to, should, or must hang it there.

Third, the so-called universalisability of value-judgments can be put in perspective and seen for what it is. Universalisability is not a peculiarity of moral judgments in particular or of practical judgments in general. It is a feature of modal judgments; and modal judgments are necessarily universalisable, i.e. imply universal principles, because they express the pressure of reason for or against something, whether doing something or thinking something. As Kant saw, it is the notion of reason that carries this feature. If the fact that p is a reason for x, it follows that any references to particular individuals in 'p' and 'x' can be eliminated in favour of universal descriptions: e.g., if the fact that Moby Dick is a whale is a conclusive reason for thinking that Moby Dick is a mammal, it follows of anything that the fact that it was a whale would be a conclusive reason for thinking that it was a mammal. In theoretical contexts, belief being transparent, the requirement of universalisability is simply the requirement of a principle of inference or argument, i.e. for a connection between premise and conclusion that is independent of any references in them to particular individuals.

4.11. *Hypothetical imperatives*

There is a fourth topic on which light is thrown by this account of modal concepts, the topic of 'hypothetical imperatives'. Since the notion of a hypothetical imperative locates a point at which the whole distinction between theoretical and practical judgments, between non-normative and normative utterances, seems particularly questionable, it has a special significance in this enquiry, and I shall therefore consider it at some length. The problem of hypothetical imperatives is precisely the problem of how apparently practical or prescriptive or normative judgments of a certain kind can be deduced, as it seems they can be, from judgments that are not themselves practical, prescriptive, or normative: e.g., from the fact that pressing the switch puts the light on, it seems to follow that if one wants to put the light on one should press the switch. Prescriptive judgments of what kind? That is part of the difficulty. The term 'hypothetical imperative' is a term of art introduced by Kant, and what exactly he meant by it is not clear enough to be unproblematic. One thing that he at least includes under this general heading is: that kind of statement saying what means to adopt to a given end, i.e. saying by what means to do a given thing. A commonplace form for such a statement is the one used above: 'If you want to do x you ought to, should, must, do y'. It is no doubt this form, which Kant himself uses, that encourages the idea that these prescriptive statements are hypothetical not only grammatically but also in logical structure; and the word 'want' in the 'antecedent' may seem to suggest that the 'obligation' referred to in the 'consequent' is conditional on feeling a desire to do the thing mentioned in the antecedent. Both of these are illusions. A less misleading formulation of a 'hypothetical imperative' is: 'To (in order to) do x A ought to, should, must do y'. Some statements of this form do not say by what means to do a certain thing, unless the word 'means' is deliberately stretched to cover them, e.g. 'To draw a triangle that can be inscribed in a semicircle one must draw a right-angle triangle'. But in that case the problem of hypothetical imperatives interpreted as statements saying by what means to do a certain thing is only one specific form of a more general problem: the problem of how prescriptive or practical statements of the form 'To do x A ought to, should, must, do y' are deducible from non-prescriptive or theoretical statements; these non-prescriptive statements, for which Hare's title is 'indicatives', including not merely statements of causal connection, which many philosophers seem to have thought of as essentially involved in the means-end relation, and not only other kinds of empirical statement, but also logically necessary or analytic statements.

The general situation is as follows. An action of one description, say x, may also be an action of another description, say y. If so, then the following weak prescriptive judgments seem to follow: 'To do x A can do y'; and 'A way (one way) to do x is to do y'. If as a matter of empirical fact or analytically only actions of description y are also actions of description x, then the following stronger prescriptive judgments follow: 'To do x A must do y' or 'The (only) way to do x is to do y'. Typical cases of this latter sort include those in which doing y is a causally or analytically necessary condition of doing x; but there are others, as in Hare's example of the fact that if Grimbly Hughes is the biggest grocer in Oxford, then to go to the biggest grocer in Oxford one must go to Grimbly Hughes. It may seem that between 'one way' and 'the only way', between what *can* be done and what *must* be done in order to do something else, lie the distinctions of worst, better, and best ways, and consequently the things not simply that can nor that must be done, but things that should or ought to be done. What is true is that these intermediate hypothetical imperatives can take the stronger form of saying what *must* be done in order to do something else, but then the considerations that exclude other possibilities will not all be purely empirical or analytic considerations, but will include, e.g., moral considerations, or considerations of prudence, and so on. More clearly, these intermediate hypothetical imperatives are not analytically deducible from statements of empirical fact or logically necessary statements. We might for this reason want to say that these are therefore not hypothetical imperatives; but that is then simply a matter of terminology.

How then is it that an apparently prescriptive type of statement, a hypothetical imperative, is deducible from an indicative? The problem arises most acutely, of course, for Hume and his followers, who approach it already armed with (or disarmed by) the general principle that 'ought' cannot be deduced from 'is'. Given this general principle, which seems to be incompatible with the apparent deducibility of hypothetical imperatives from indicatives, one obvious way of reconciliation is to deny that the relation is one of strict deducibility or entailment; and another is to admit the entailment and deny that hypothetical imperatives really are, as they seem to be, prescriptive at all.

One thing that is clear is that not all statements of the form 'To do x A must (or can) do y' are practical judgments in my sense, and are therefore not hypothetical imperatives in the sense in which that term is usually understood. It should by now come as no surprise to discover that in this case also, though the modal words 'can' and 'must' have a normative function, their occurrence is not sufficient to make the judgments in which they occur *practical* judgments; for the displacement that is characteristic of theoretical contexts associates them with descriptions of items on which they do not bear normatively. Thus it might be said, for instance, that to flood the town the river must rise at least three feet, or that to uproot a tree the wind must reach gale force. Since the river and the wind are not the sort of agents for which the question of what to do, and in particular the question of what to do in order to do something else, can arise, these statements cannot be answers to that practical question; and in them the

word 'must' signifies the pressure of reason in favour of an answer
not to that question but to the theoretical question of what would
have to be true of the river given that it were to flood the town, and
of the wind, given that it were to uproot a tree. The presence of
the word 'want' in the more usual formulation of a hypothetical
imperative, i.e. in the formulation 'If A wants to do x A must (or
can) do y', can be seen as ruling out this theoretical interpretation
and indicating that this is a genuine hypothetical imperative, an
answer to the practical question of what to do in order to do x.
But a counterpart theoretical statement of the form 'To do x A
must do y', i.e. a statement in which the 'must' introduces an
empirically or analytically necessary condition, will also be true
of agents for whom the practical question does arise, and it is
from such a theoretical statement that the practical hypothetical
imperative can be regarded as deducible. However, it may now
seem that to talk of there being two statements, one of them
empirical or analytic, the other prescriptive or practical, this latter
being deducible from the former, is itself partly responsible for the
problem of hypothetical imperatives: for the situation is less misleadingly described as follows, that given that A is an agent for
whom the question of what to do arises, a theoretical statement of
the form 'To do x A must do y' has a practical interpretation,
answering A's question of what to do in order to do x. The change
in interpretation involves a change in point of view, and a
consequent shift of the normative force of the modal word onto
that item with whose description it is grammatically associated,
namely doing y.

But is a hypothetical imperative then really a practical judgment? Is it really the case that the normative force of the modal
word has a practical bearing, on that action the description of
which it introduces? We face here a dilemma. In 4.7 I argued that
practical judgments are such that it is possible for one's actions to
be inconsistent with what one thinks one should do. Now it is, of
course, possible for someone to think that to do x he must do y
and yet not do y when the occasion arises. But when does the
occasion arise? In both its theoretical and practical interpretation
this word 'must', like the words 'consistent' and 'entails', connects
two items: the hypothetical imperative does not say that A must
do y, but only that A must do y *in order to do x*. It looks then as if,
for someone's action to be inconsistent with his judgment that in
order to do x he must do y, it would be necessary for him not

merely not to do y but also to do x. The modal connection, one might say, is between doing x and doing y, such that doing y is required or necessary only because doing x requires or necessitates it. But in that case the hypothetical imperative cannot be in practice contravened: the possibility of contravention is ruled out by the very statement, the theoretical counterpart of the hypothetical imperative, from which that imperative is 'deduced', the statement, that is, that to do x one must do y, i.e. that one cannot do x without doing y. Thus, we may conclude, since the hypothetical imperative cannot be contravened by any action on the part of the agent, it is not genuinely imperative, prescriptive, or in my sense practical: the modal connection between doing x and doing y is theoretical only, and does not bear normatively on doing y.[1]

It is to be noted that this argument showing that hypothetical imperatives are not practically contravenable is independent of whether or not the person whose action is in question knows or thinks that to do x he must do y. In other words, it is independent of the consideration involved in Hare's prescriptivism, which claims that if A thinks that he should or must do y then necessarily A will do y if and when the occasion arises. Hare's position is that in general A's conduct can contravene the judgment that he should or must do y—provided that that judgment is not A's judgment: if it is A who thinks that he should do y, then A's conduct cannot contravene that judgment. The argument above about hypothetical imperatives shows that even if the judgment that to do x A must do y is not A's judgment, A's conduct cannot contravene such a judgment.

Is this Hare's own view of hypothetical imperatives? This is certainly a possible interpretation. He sums up his account as follows: 'It would probably be misleading to say that hypothetical imperatives are "really indicatives" . . . The best way of describing the matter has been suggested by Kant: the imperative element in an hypothetical imperative is analytic ("who wills the end . . . wills also the means"), because the imperatives in the two parts, so to say, cancel one another out. It is an imperative, but *qua* imperative, has no content; the content which it has is that of the indicative . . . from which it is derived'.[2] This interpretation is supported by the idea that imperative logic is isomorphous with

[1] cf. Kant's Second Remark, and its footnote, on Theorem I, § II, of the Analytic in the *Critique of Practical Reason*.
[2] op. cit., pp. 36–7.

propositional logic, at least as far as the propositional calculus goes, obedience-conditions playing, with respect to imperatives, a role analogous to that of truth-conditions for indicatives. The theory of hypothetical imperatives would then be that given the indicative from which such an imperative is derived, it is logically impossible for it to be contravened ('falsified') by anybody's actions, and it is therefore, as an imperative, analytic or tautologous. This is true in the sense outlined. Hare contends that both clauses of a hypothetical imperative are imperatives: taking as his example of a hypothetical imperative the statement 'If you want to go to the largest grocer in Oxford, go to Grimbly Hughes', which follows from 'Grimbly Hughes is the largest grocer in Oxford', he claims that ' "want" is here a logical term, and stands . . . for an imperative inside a subordinate clause'.[1] The hypothetical imperative thus means what, if it were English, would be meant by 'If go to the largest grocer in Oxford, go to Grimbly Hughes'. Given the fact from which this is deduced, no action or combination of actions can contravene this imperative, i.e. one cannot both fulfil the antecedent clause and not fulfil the consequent clause: it must be obeyed. Who achieves the end must perform the means.

Unfortunately for this interpretation, it results in a theory that can only doubtfully claim, as Hare claims, Kant's support. In Hare's quotation from Kant, as Hare himself correctly indicates, something is omitted. One of Kant's versions of the analytic principle governing the form of all hypothetical imperatives is: 'whoever wills the end, wills also (so far as reason decides his conduct) the means . . .'.[2] Is it this parenthesis that Hare's quotation omits? But that parenthesis contains a qualification that clearly distinguishes Kant's view from the interpretation of Hare's theory outlined above. For that qualification implies that reason may in fact not decide one's conduct, and therefore that, as a matter of fact, whoever wills the end may *not* will the means. It is of course indicatively true, in the words summarising the argument of the preceding paragraph, that who *achieves* the end must *perform* the means. But Kant's word is 'wills', and in his view, therefore, there must be some distinction to be drawn between *willing* the end and the means and actually *doing* those things

[1] op. cit., p. 34.
[2] Second section of the *Fundamental Principles of the Metaphysic of Morals*, translated by T. K. Abbott.

whose descriptions occur in the two clauses of a hypothetical imperative: a distinction which, while ruling out the possibility that somebody should achieve the end without performing the means, nevertheless allows the possibility that somebody should will the end without willing the means. This distinction may hold the clue to the difference between the theoretical and practical interpretations of statements of the form 'To do x A must do y', and may therefore show how the normative force of the modal word in the theoretical interpretation can come to have a practical bearing.

It is not difficult to see that this distinction must be drawn if statements of this form are to have a practical interpretation. What is essential to this interpretation is that such a statement should be an answer to an agent's question of what to do, in particular to an agent's question of what to do in order to do something else. This question and this answer, therefore, must have a possible role in an agent's deliberations about what to do in order to do something else, i.e. a possible role in a setting in which the agent has not yet done that something else but has decided to do it, or intends to do it, or has the purpose or aim of doing it, in brief, using a familiar sense of the word, in a setting in which the agent *wants* to do that something else, and needs to know what to do in order to do that other thing. It is in this sense that the word 'want' occurs in hypothetical imperatives. If we say, with Hare, that this word 'stands . . . for an imperative' we shall have to say, against Hare, that in intending to do something we can either assent to an imperative without doing what it enjoins, or accept an imperative without assenting to it in his sense. Of course somebody can intend to do something without doing, and even without intending to do, what he must do in order to do that thing: unlike a river or the wind, agents of which it may be true that to do x they must do y, human agents, of which such a thing may also be true, can will the end without willing the means. Though for both human and natural agents it is doing x that requires or necessitates doing y, it is only in the human case that intending (wanting) to do x normatively requires or necessitates doing y. Thus human agents can fail to do what they normatively must do, can by their conduct contravene a hypothetical imperative.

One way in which contravention of a hypothetical imperative can occur is in the situation in which, though A intends to do x

and must do y in order to do x, A does not do y because he does
not know or think that in order to do what he intends he must do
y. It might be thought that it is the possibility of this situation that
answers to Hare's account, though it is clearly different from the
interpretation suggested earlier; and it was perhaps this possibility
that Hare himself had in mind as answering to the principle he
quotes from Kant. Certainly, given that a hypothetical imperative
is understood as having an antecedent clause that is not an
imperative in Hare's sense, Hare's prescriptivism, applied to his
contention that the consequent clause is also an imperative,
would imply that if someone intended to do x and thought or
knew that to do x he must do y, then it would follow necessarily
that he would do y if and when the occasion arose. On this view,
the situation outlined in the opening sentence of this paragraph
would be the only one in which a hypothetical imperative could be
contravened; and in Kant's language, supplying the missing
parenthesis in Hare's quotation, the only way in which reason
could fail to decide an agent's conduct in this context.

Even for this claim, however, Kant's support is doubtful, to say
the least. Hypothetical imperatives are a species of imperatives,
and Kant's account of imperatives in general, before his division
of them into two species, maintains that imperatives hold for the
human and not for a holy will precisely because for a human agent
'actions which objectively are *recognised* as necessary are subjec-
tively contingent',[1] so that 'all imperatives . . . say that something
would be good to do or to forbear, but they say it to a will which
does not always do a thing because it is *conceived* to be good to do
it'.[2] The implication is that the situation described at the beginning
of the preceding paragraph is not the only one in which a human
agent may contravene a hypothetical imperative: reason may fail
to decide his conduct in this way too, that he may not do y even
though he intends to do x and thinks or knows that to do x he
must do y. If this is the case, my argument in 4.7 applies equally
to hypothetical imperatives and shows them to be practical
judgments in that sense: one's conduct can be inconsistent with
one's judgment that to do x one must do y. It seems to me that this
is the case. Weakness of will is possible in this situation, and constitutes a more radical breakdown of rationality in conduct than
the other case, in which the agent who fails to do what he must do

[1] Second section of the *Fundamental Principles* (my italics).
[2] ibid. (my italics).

in order to do what he intends is merely ignorant of this necessity.[1]

To conclude this discussion, a possible misunderstanding must be eliminated. It might be thought that it follows from my account that if to do x A must do y, then the following statement is true, that if A intends to x, he must do y, and this is a hypothetical in the formal logicians' sense in which a rule of detachment applies to it, so that the truth of the antecedent allows us to detach the consequent and assert its truth categorically. This would be a *reductio ad absurdum* of my account, since it would imply, e.g., that the practical judgment that Smith must set fire to Grimbly Hughes would be justified simply on the grounds that Smith intends to set fire to the biggest grocer in Oxford and that to set fire to the biggest grocer in Oxford he must set fire to Grimbly Hughes. Fortunately, my argument has no such implication.

To show this, and to sum up some of the chief points of the foregoing discussion, let us suppose that to do x A must do y. Then we have the following theoretical implications:

(T1) If A does, or did, or will do, x, A must do, or must have done, y.

(T2) If A does, or did, or will do, x, that fact is a (conclusive) reason for thinking that A does, or did, or will do, y.

(T3) If it is right to think that A does, or did, or will do, x, one must think that A does, or did, or will do, y.

(T4) If one thinks that A does, or did, or will do, x, one must (in consistency) think that A does, or did, or will do, y.

Given that A is a human agent for whom the question can arise of what to do in order to do x, we have the following practical implications:

(P1) If A wants to do x he must do y.

(P2) If do x, do y.

(P3) If A wants to do x he wants to do y.

(P4) If A is right to do x he is right to do y.

(P5) If A must, should, or ought to, do x, he must, should, or ought to, do y.

(P6) If A is right to intend to do x he must intend to do y.

(P7) If A intends (wills) to do x he must (in consistency) intend (will) to do y.

(P8) If A intends to do x he must (in consistency) do y.

[1] cf. Sidgwick's *The Methods of Ethics* (Macmillan, London, 1907), pp. 36–38.

(P1) is the normal and traditional formulation of a hypothetical imperative. (P2) is Hare's version. (P3), (P4), and (P5) all answer to one aspect or another of Hume's account of the role of reason in action, though (P3) would not appear in my list of implications if it were construed as Hume would apparently construe it, according to his view that when we have a desire for an object (e.g. to do x) 'these emotions extend themselves to the causes and effects of that object, as they are pointed out to us by reason and experience'.[1] Hare's doctrine that in (P2) the imperative element is analytic assimilates hypothetical imperatives either to these Humean hypotheticals or to (T1), which is not a practical (imperative) implication at all. My account in effect draws attention to (P6), (P7), and (P8).

(T2), (T3), and (T4) make explicit the theoretical bearing of the normative force of the modal word 'must'. (P6) is a practical counterpart of (T3), and (P7) of (T4). For (P6) and (P7) are versions of those special forms of (T3) and (T4) in which it is A who is thinking about his doing x and doing y, and the thinking is future-tense. In these forms, the readings are:

> ($T3_p$) If A is right to think that he will do x, he must think that he will do y.
> ($T4_p$) If A thinks that he will do x he must (in consistency) think that he will do y.

When A's thinking that he will do x is practical thinking, i.e. the kind of thinking that is intending, ($T3_p$) and ($T4_p$) are indistinguishable from (P6) and (P7) respectively.

It is to be noticed that in (T3) and ($T3_p$), and in (P4), (P5), and (P6), antecedents as well as consequents are normative, evaluative, or prescriptive; whereas in (T4) and (T4p), and in (P7) and (P8), the normative consequents have non-normative antecedents. It is for this reason that, given the truth of these non-normative antecedents, these normative consequents are not detachable in accordance with the rule of detachment—unless the parenthesis is included. For the function of that parenthesis is to imply that the pressure of reason expressed by the modal word 'must' in these contexts is that pressure exerted by the requirement of consistency; and this requirement is a comparatively weak one in this sense, that being consistent is not enough for being right, i.e. of two con-

[1] op. cit., p. 414.

sistent items, either or both may be wrong. Without the parenthesis, explicit or understood, the detached consequent would not allow for this possibility. To put the matter crudely, we may say that the normative force of a hypothetical imperative bears not on the end, nor, given the end, on the means itself, but only on the means in relation to the end. Though it may be the case that A intends to do x, and that to do x he must do y, it may also be the case that (all things considered) he should not do y: if so, it will of course also follow that he should not do, or intend to do, x. This is why, as practical judgments, hypothetical imperatives are best represented by (P7), which is Kant's principle, and (P8), which implies and is implied by (P7).

4.12. *The explanatory role of a person's reasons*

In 4.2 I said that philosophers who have held that a reason for doing something is not a species of reason coordinate with a reason for believing that something is the case have sometimes held that a reason for doing something is a cause of doing it, a motive or desire. I have argued so far that it is logically normative, and in this respect similar to a reason for believing something. Does this exclude the other view?

Clearly, for the idea of a reason for doing something even to be a candidate for specifying a causal relation between the reason and the action it is a reason for, that action must be something actually done. If the question of whether to do x arises for someone, it may be that the fact that p is a reason for him to do x, or a reason he has for doing x; but he may still not do x, however conclusive or sufficient the reasons he has for doing it. Similarly, he may be said to want to do x, or to have a motive for doing it, without actually doing it. However, when he does x, and *his* reason for doing x is that p, is it then the case that his reason, namely the fact that p, is what caused him to do x? We may say, e.g., that he did it because p, or because he thought that p, and this word 'because' seems to introduce a causal explanation of his doing x: these statements are of the general causal form 'p because q', e.g. the window broke because the stone struck it. Any statement of this form may be said to assert that the fact that q is the reason why p, or that the reason why p is that q, and this is no less true when the statement is of the more specific form 'A did x because q'.

Some statements of this more specific form are causal statements in which the fact that q, though the reason why A did x, is not A's

reason for doing x, e.g. 'He sneezed because he had a cold'. What
further conditions must hold for the fact that q to be A's reason
for doing x? 'A's reason for doing x was that q' has two implications that 'The reason why A did x was that q' does not have: it
implies 'A knew or thought that q' and also 'A did x intentionally'.
It is in virtue of the former implication that when a statement of
the form 'A did x because q' gives A's reason for having done x,
this statement also implies 'A did x because A thought (or knew)
that q'. Unless A thought or knew that q, that q, though perhaps a
reason he had for doing x, could not be his reason for doing x.
When someone says that A did x because A thought that q, such
a statement reveals what A's reason was for having done x, but it
does so without commitment on two questions, one of which A
must have been committed on, the other of which he may have
been committed on. It is uncommitted, as A cannot have been, on
the question whether q, and it is uncommitted, as A may not have
been, on the question whether, if it were a fact that q, that fact
would have been a (good) reason for A to have done x. In other
words, A, in saying 'I did x because q', is committing himself to
the claim that q, and may be offering the alleged fact that q as a
justification of his having done x. B (or A himself) in saying 'A did
x because A thought that q', commits himself on neither matter.
B's statement is, so to speak, a purely descriptive version of A's:
it is A's statement without the normative implications for A's
having done x. It depicts in profile, from the point of view of a
neutral observer, the working of A's reason with respect to his
having done x. In this way, B's statement fulfils one requirement
of a causal explanation of A's having done x: like the causal
explanation of the window's having broken, it speaks neither in
favour of nor against the item it explains; and its relation to A's
having done x is thus very different from that of the statement that
the fact that q is a reason for doing x.

There is a second way in which B's statement qualifies as a
causal explanation of A's having done x. The statement that A did
x because he thought that q implies that A would not have done x
if he had not thought that q. Is this true only if we add 'in those
circumstances', i.e. only if we suppose all the other circumstances
to remain the same? Or is it true regardless of those other circumstances, so that it implies that even if the other circumstances had
been different, if A had not thought that q he would not have done
x? It seems clear that this latter interpretation is unacceptable.

Let us consider an example. Suppose that Smith took his coat because he thought that the weather was cold. It might be that Smith would have taken his coat even if he had not thought that the weather was cold, provided some of the other circumstances had been different, e.g. that he had had a fever, or that he had thought that it was going to rain. On the other hand, he might also still have taken his coat if all the other circumstances had remained the same; for one of these other circumstances might have been his thinking that without his coat he would feel cold, and if that circumstance had remained the same he might have taken his coat, even though he did not think that the weather was cold. However, though perhaps 'logically' (i.e. analytically) possible, the supposition that this condition requires us to make, that of a situation similar to the actual situation in all respects except one, is in this context unintelligible and cannot therefore be the basis of an enquiry into whether in such circumstances Smith would have done the same thing. What is not unintelligible is to suppose that if Smith had not thought that the weather was cold some other circumstances, though not all, would also have been different in consequence; and the implication of the statement that A did x because he thought that q, is that if A had not thought that q (and consequently if some other circumstances had been different) he would not have done x.

One of the ways of preserving this principle against the objection that even if, in our example, Smith had not thought that the weather was cold he would still have taken his coat, is thus to represent the explanation as incomplete and requiring expansion in terms of the other circumstances that would consequently differ under the supposition. The unintelligiblity of supposing that all the other circumstances remain the same, including the one that explains why he would still take his coat, namely his thinking that without it he would feel cold, is precisely that the original explanation requires some such factor as this if it is to be expanded into a fuller explanation. How exactly is this factor to be fitted in to make the explanation more complete? Hume raises the question whether reason alone can motivate action, and his answer is that something else is needed to explain intentional conduct, a passion, desire, or emotion. But in my example the incompleteness of the explanation simply reflects the incompleteness of the statement of Smith's reasons for taking his coat. More specifically, it reflects the derivativeness of the reason given. In Smith's view, we may say, the fact that the weather was cold was a reason for taking a coat only because this fact was causally connected with this other, that without a coat he would have felt cold; or more generally, the fact that the weather was cold was a reason only because, that being so, he would have felt cold without a coat, and in Smith's view it was this fact that was the more basic reason for taking a coat. Thus the fuller explanation of Smith's having taken his coat would be as follows: Smith took his coat because he thought that without it he would feel cold, and he thought this because he thought that the weather was cold. The implication of this explanation is that if he had not thought that the weather was cold the other circumstances would not have remained the same; for he would not have thought that without his coat he would have felt cold. We can construct this fuller explanation of Smith's action by reconstructing the argument in which Smith's reasons figure as considerations leading to a decision or intention on his part to perform that action: 'The weather's cold; so if I don't take a coat I shall feel cold; so I shall take a coat'. This rational reconstruction does not, of course, imply that Smith actually argued in this way, to himself or to anyone else, or that he consciously rehearsed these considerations in his mind before taking his coat. What it does is to bring out the way in which one reason depends on another, and thus how an explanation of Smith's action in terms of one of his beliefs depends on the way in which that belief explains another of his beliefs. Thus the condition of other circumstances remaining the same is subject to this restriction, that it does not apply to those other beliefs that the original one both explains and requires in the rational reconstruction of the practical argument leading to the action. It is because Smith's thinking that the weather is cold explains not only his taking his coat but also his thinking that if he doesn't take his coat he will feel cold, and explains the former through the latter, that if he had not thought that the weather was cold he would neither have thought that without a coat he would feel cold nor, therefore, have taken his coat.

It needs to be added that this is not a peculiarity of the way in which an agent's reasons explain his conduct, but a characteristic of any causal explanation. Constant heavy traffic may cause a building to collapse. This does not imply that if there had not been constant heavy traffic, all other circumstances remaining the same, the building would not have collapsed; for one of those other circumstances may have been that the foundations were weakened by vibration until they could no longer support the superstructure, and if that had remained the same the building would still have collapsed. But if that is so, this factor must be required by the original explanation, which could therefore be expanded into the fuller explanation 'Constant heavy traffic caused the building to collapse by shaking its foundations until they were too weak to support the superstructure'.

Can we then say that when someone's reason for doing x was that q, the statement that he did x because he thought that q is a causal explanation of his having done x? One important consideration seems to count against this view. Causal explanations, at least in many typical and central cases, require for their support inductive evidence of a regular correlation between cause and effect; whereas a statement to the effect that A did x because he thought that q, where the alleged fact that q was A's reason for doing x, does not require an inductively established regularity in which things done of the kind x are correlated with the agent's thinking such things as that q. A himself can say what his reasons were without basing his claim on any such inductive regularity; and it is because this is so that even for another person, B, the centre of the evidence for his claim that A did x because he thought that q is again not an inductively established correlation between these two items, but the fact that A himself says that his reason was that q. I am not, of course, claiming that if A does not say what his reason was B cannot find out by other means what it was; nor that if A does say that his reason was that q then it necessarily follows that he did x because he thought that q. My point is simply that on this matter A's words have an authority that they could not have if they or anybody else's words to the same effect required support from the inductive evidence of a regular correlation.

Does this show that statements of the sort we are considering are not causal statements? I shall say that it does, though once we are clear about the similarities and differences I do not think that much hangs on which way we decide. We can divide into these two species either the genus of causal explanations, so that some are inductive and some are not, or the genus of explanations, so that some are causal and some are not. Either way it is clear that 'A did x because he thought that q' does not justify A's having done x but does explain why he did it.

This pattern of explanation connected with the normative notion of reason is not peculiar to practical reason but is equally characteristic of theoretical reason. If the fact that p is a reason for thinking that q it may be A's reason for thinking that q; and it will then be the case, in explanatory terms that speak neither in favour of nor against his thinking that q, that A thinks that q because he thinks that p. As I have already explained, in the practical case the counterpart explanation is uncommitted on two matters, one of which A must be and one of which he may be committed on, namely whether p and whether the fact that p is a good reason. In the theoretical case these two matters answer to the two conditions which, as I said in 1.1, must hold if an argument is to establish its conclusion: in presenting his reason for thinking that q in the form of an argument, 'p, so q', A commits himself both to the truth of the proposition that p and to the validity or acceptability of the inference, i.e. to the claim that the fact that p is a (good or conclusive) reason for thinking that q.

In general, reason, in whatever field, must have an explanatory role in this sense: if the fact that p is a reason for doing x (in a wide sense of 'do'), the fact that p must be capable of being somebody's reason for doing x; and if it is somebody's reason for doing x it must be the case that that person does, did, or will do x because he thinks or thought that p. The doing of things that people in this wide sense do is, as is well known, an area of complicated interplay between the normative role of reason, the explanatory role of reason, and causal explanation.

5

THE FACULTY OF REASON

5.1. *The general nature of reason*

My aim so far has been to describe and explain some of the chief similarities and differences between theoretical and practical reason, showing in the process that scepticism about practical reason has been the result of misconceiving these similarities and differences. What I want to do in this last chapter is to consolidate the case against scepticism by drawing together the main threads of the argument into a pattern that reveals in outline the general nature of reason and so, by locating the sources of the similarities and differences, enables us to preserve the insights without the distortions of the sceptical position.

The idea of the general nature of reason that emerges from the foregoing chapters is a traditional idea, but one that corrects some important misconceptions, sometimes made explicit but persistently suggested and encouraged, by much rationalist writing in philosophy and logic. Under the influence of these misconceptions reason itself is thought of as a source of information in somewhat the way in which sense-experience or perception is a source of information: it is a light that reveals, or like sight a faculty that discovers, truths about reality, truths that supplement, or perhaps even compete with, what we seem to learn from our senses. It is against this view that empiricism reacts with its characteristic doctrines that these alleged truths of reason are empty, uninformative, not about reality, simply linguistic.

As my arguments suggest, the notion of truths of reason (including, e.g., so-called 'logical truths') has a place in any full account of reason, as does the connection between such truths and linguistic rules. But both these matters, each of which has constituted part of the one-sided diet of rationalists on the one hand and empiricists on the other, need to be seen for what they are, aspects of reason, not the whole of it or even its most central features. The idea of the general nature of reason that has taken shape in the course of my arguments is that reason is a mental faculty whose essential function is the normative one of directing or guiding other human faculties; and it is in relation to this function that truths of reason and linguistic rules must be understood. Figuratively, the focus of reason's interest is not 'the external world' but the things that people in a broad sense do: at these points reason brings pressure to bear, and though they include, they are not exhausted by, people's utterances. The existence of truths of reason may seem to be incompatible with this, but this is an illusion due to the transparency of belief.

The explanation of my choice of the concept of a reason for or against something as one of the central concepts in the family of concepts of reason is now clear. It is in the idea that the fact that p is a reason for or against doing something (in a broad sense of 'do'), and in the idea that the fact that p is somebody's reason for doing something, that we have both the notion of the faculty of reason and the notion of those faculties directed by it, the faculties designated by the categories of verbal nouns ranged over by the variable 'doing something', namely belief, action, and passion. The view that there is a single faculty of reason that is exercised in different ways is the view that through the differences there is a group of essential characteristics that remain invariant: in particular a reason is a fact that bears normatively on what it is a reason for and can explain someone's 'doing' what it is a reason for 'doing'. Given this pattern of relations, it seems natural and obvious to conjecture that the differences between one exercise of reason and another, e.g. between theoretical and practical reason, are due to differences between the faculties subordinate to it, e.g. between belief and action.

These two ideas, of the invariant normative and explanatory roles of reason, and of the different ways in which these roles are fulfilled in respect of the different faculties it directs, are closely connected. The notion of reason presupposes the notion of other faculties, and of the possible exercise of these other faculties

independently of reason. This possibility shapes both the normative and the explanatory role, and brings them together into
intelligible relation. In giving an account of these matters I shall
be extracting from its sceptical context the core of truth in Hume's
claim that reason alone is not sufficient, that of itself reason is
'utterly impotent', 'perfectly inert', 'wholly inactive'.

5.2. *Presuppositions of reasons for believing*

Let us, by way of introduction to the topic, return to the common
idea, made explicit by Hume, that reason is essentially connected
with truth in the sense that it 'discovers' or 'produces' truths. It is
of course the case that in the idea that the fact that p is a reason
for believing that q the concept of reason is connected with the
truth of the assertion that q. But this is because, in this theoretical
context, the reason is a reason for *believing* something: it is the
faculty of belief, not that of reason, that is as such essentially
connected in this way with truth. Moreover, as I argued in 3.21,
the connection between reason and truth here is mediated by the
evaluative notion of its being right or correct to believe this or
that: the idea of its being true that p entails that it is right or
correct to think that p, and wrong or mistaken to think that *not-p*,
i.e. the question whether p, which may be an empirical question, is
analytically connected with the evaluative question of whether it
is right to think that p. This connection is of the type discussed in
3.16 and 3.17: the fact that p is normatively related to the belief
that p, but not by being a reason for believing that p. The normative notion of something's being a reason for believing that p
presupposes· this more basic mode of appraising belief. The
normative character of reason in general is differentiated in
its relation to belief by this presupposed mode of appraisal
peculiar to the faculty of belief. The presupposed notion is that
of something that it is correct to believe where the correctness of the belief is not a matter of there being reasons for
believing it.

Ultimately, this more basic mode of appraising belief must be
in terms of its conformity or otherwise with experience, e.g. sense-
perception. I shall not argue for this empiricist claim, but the view
gains plausibility from the fact that there is an analytic connection
between the concepts of experience and correctly believing something at the level at which believing that thing is not justifiable or
explicable by reference to reasons. There are various ways of

identifying someone's experience, e.g. his perceptual impressions. We may say that he experiences something as green, or that it appears or seems or looks to him to be green, or that he has a visual impression as of something green. Some philosophers have held that experience in this sense is a substratum presupposed by but distinguishable from judgment or belief or thought: a sort of raw material from which thoughts, concepts, and judgments are manufactured. A more plausible account has been given by G. N. A. Vesey: 'What an object looks like to somebody is what on looking at it, that person would take it to be, if he had no reason to think otherwise'.[1] I would say: 'It looks green to him' entails 'He would judge or think it to be green unless there were something that was his reason for thinking otherwise'. Thus someone to whom something looked green, and who took no account of (actual or possible) reasons against thinking it green, would necessarily think that it was green. In these circumstances, its looking green to him would explain his belief by ruling out such alternative explanations as that he inferred that it was green. But it would not explain his belief either causally or by giving his reason; for the belief and the experience explaining it would not in this case be analytically independent. We have here that exercise of the faculty of belief presupposed by the notion of a reason for believing something: if there are no reasons against such a belief it must be true and therefore correct to believe it; and someone's believing it in such a case is not explicable in terms of his reasons.

Seen in this light, Hume's dictum that reason of itself is 'utterly impotent' has an application to theoretical reason as well as to practical reason, but its sceptical implications are quite properly directed at the pretentious claims made for reason by the rationalist philosophers, not, as Hume mistakenly draws them in his argument against practical reason, at the ordinary (i.e. nonphilosophical) notion of reason itself. The application is simply that there could be no such thing as a reason for believing something unless there were cases in which it was both correct and possible to believe something without reasons; and these are cases in which experience takes over the normative and explanatory role of reason with respect to belief.

[1] 'Seeing and Seeing As', *Proceedings of the Aristotelian Society*, vol. LVI, 1955–6. See also Vesey's 'Sensations of Colour' in *Mill: A Collection of Critical Essays*, Ed. by J. B. Schneewind.

5.3. *Doing and wanting*

Does the notion of a reason for doing something (in a narrow sense of 'do') have an analogous pattern of presuppositions? I shall argue that it does have, though with some key differences. My argument takes up a suggestion that has recurred in philosophical discussions of the topic: that in important ways the notion of wanting something functions in the practical field analogously to that of experience in the theoretical field.

The first thing to note is a resemblance. Just as experience is not a causal precondition of belief but is analytically connected with it, so wanting to do something, which has often been thought of as a causal precondition of doing that thing, is rather analytically connected with doing it. Anscombe has said: 'The primitive sign of wanting is *trying to get . . .*'.[1] In what sense is it a 'primitive sign'? Among those things about which the question arises of whether to do them, anything that someone wants to do will be what he will do, or try to do, unless there is something that is his reason for doing otherwise. Analogously with the relation between experience and belief this does not imply that there is any reason to do such a thing or that if he does it the agent does it for some reason.

Secondly, wanting to do something is analytically connected not only with doing that thing, but also with the appraisal of conduct (again, see Anscombe):[2] wanting something to some degree and in some way involves thinking or knowing it to be good to that degree and in that way.

Third, a difference: one can have a reason for wanting something, but not a reason for experiencing something in a certain way. Now when one has a reason for wanting something, and what one wants is to do something, the reason one has for wanting to do that thing is also a reason for doing it. The word 'want' in this context seems to signify little more than the explanatory power of reason, and it does this by virtue of the first point just made, the parallel between wanting and experience. For if A wants to do x and his reason for wanting to do x is that p, then A will do or try to do x unless he has reason to do otherwise; and if he does x, the explanation of his doing it will be not 'because he wanted to' but in terms of his reason, i.e. 'because he thought that p'.

[1] op. cit., p. 67.
[2] esp. op. cit., p. 75.

5.4. *Wanting without reason*

It is, however, possible to want something when it is not the case that there is some fact that is one's reason for wanting it. Hume could be represented as holding that if in the ordinary sense we have a reason for doing something, this implies that we have a reason for wanting to do that thing, which in its turn implies that there is something that we want without reason, i.e. when it is not the case that we have a reason for wanting it; and that if we have no reason for wanting to do something of a certain description, we have no reason for doing it, and do it, if at all, just because we want to: so that a so-called reason for doing something is really a reason only for thinking that something is the case. But there are two (at least two) different kinds of situation that might be covered by the idea of wanting something when it is not the case that there is something that is one's reason for wanting it. There is, first, the kind of situation in which we do something intentionally, knowing what we are doing, but doing the thing, as we say, on impulse, or on a sudden whim, or just because we feel like it, or want to. There is, on the other hand, the kind of case that was uppermost in Hume's mind: the kind of case in which we have a reason for wanting something, namely because it is a means to something else that we want 'in itself' or 'as an end' and therefore for no reason; e.g. happiness, pleasure, or enjoyment.

It is in the former kind of case that the agent is least misleadingly described as doing the thing *because* he wanted to. But what exactly is the force of this explanation? In particular, what is its relation to the idea of an agent's reasons for doing something? Traditionally it seems to have been thought that reason is always distinguishable from, and even opposed to, wanting, desire, or inclination. But this may have been due, in part at least, to the usual exaggerated importance accorded by philosophers to what they have considered to be their own kind of reason, theoretical reason: certainly 'A believes that p because he wants to' does not give A's reason for believing that p, though it may well be true as an explanation.[1] So far as action is concerned, to the extent that an explanation of the sort 'A did x because he wanted to' is of the

---

[1] It is a curious fact that the topic of 'the conflict between reason and passion' has been so pervasive in philosophical discussions of practice but almost completely ignored in philosophical discussions of theory. There is an important insight in this discrimination, but rather more prejudice.

form '*A* did *x* because *q*' that form itself contains nothing that stamps the explanation as causal rather than as an explanation in terms of *A*'s reasons. In normal contexts, an explanation of this sort carries both implications distinctive of explanations in terms of the agent's reasons: it implies both '*A* did *x* intentionally' and '*A* knew or thought that he wanted to do *x*'. In cases in which *A* both does *x* and wants to do *x* the failure of the former implication is enough to rule out the possibility that the fact that he wanted to was his reason, and with it the possibility that his wanting to in any way explains why he did *x*: e.g. when *A* wants to sneeze and sneezes. It might be thought that the fact that one wants to do something is no reason for doing it, and therefore that explanation in terms of the agent's wants is not explanation in terms of his reasons. But this is a confusion. To say that some fact is no reason for doing something is compatible with saying that it was the agent's reason for doing that thing: the implication is that his reason was a bad reason for doing it. Is this implication correct for the situation in which someone, doing something on impulse, is said to do it 'just because he wants to'?

I do not think that it is. The force of the explanation is precisely to reject the idea that there is something that was the agent's reason, while allowing that the action, being intentional, was of a sort such that there could have been something that was his reason for doing it. The answer to the question 'What was your reason for doing that?' would in this case quite properly be 'No reason. I just wanted to' or 'I just felt like it'. As Anscombe has said:[1] 'The question is not refused application because the answer to it says that there is *no* reason, any more than the question how much money I have in my pocket is refused application by the answer "None"'. Having no reason in this kind of case is not to be confused with having no reason in the situation in which one does something accidentally, or by mistake, or not realising that one is doing it, etc.

5.5. *Ultimate wants and reasons for doing things*

It seems likely that this genuine case of there being nothing that is the agent's reason either for wanting to do something or for doing it has been confused with the kind of case in which explanation of conduct involves reference to 'ultimate' desires, i.e. to things that are wanted in themselves, not as means to something else or

[1] op. cit., p. 25.

for any other reason. But there are important differences. One is that it is not true that in explanations of this latter kind we reach an action of some description that the agent did because he wanted to. Certainly we may reach a description of something that the agent wants, and it may be something, such as happiness or enjoyment, that he wants without there being some fact that is his reason for wanting it. It does not follow that his wanting it is irrational or unreasonable; nor does it follow that the fact that he would enjoy doing something cannot be his reason for doing it. The pattern of conceptual relationships here is complicated and obscure but the following account seems to me to be correct in broad outline.

There are some things that we want, and therefore think or rather know to be good, not just as a contingent matter of fact but necessarily, e.g. happiness. This means that if the question arises for someone of whether to do x, the fact that he thinks he would enjoy doing x implies that in some way and to some degree he wants to do x. Other facts have similar relations to wanting to do things: for instance, the fact that one feels tired implies that one wants to rest, and the fact that one feels hungry or thirsty implies that one wants to eat or drink. Now not only people but (other) animals can want things, enjoy things, feel tired, hungry, thirsty, and so on; and if an animal is without the use of reason, what it at any moment wants to do is necessarily what it will do if it can. This notion of wanting to do a certain thing, and its related notions of doing that thing and of thinking that it would be a good thing to do, are presupposed by the concept of a reason for doing something. The applicability of this concept requires in addition an agent capable of knowing, believing, thinking, or realising that this or that is the case, and of bearing in mind at one and the same time matters of such a sort that his consequent wants could be incompatible, i.e. of such a sort that he could want to do x and want to do y, where doing one would make it impossible for him to do the other. In this situation of possible (though not necessarily actual) conflict of wants, an agent's reason for doing x is that fact his belief in which entails that he wants to do x. At this basic level, that fact, if it is a fact, is not only *his* reason for doing x it is also *a* reason for doing x: he may be mistaken about whether he would enjoy doing x, or is tired, or hungry; but he cannot be mistaken in regarding these facts, if they are facts, as reasons for doing x, or resting, or eating. This incorrigibility is simply a reflection of our knowing happiness to be good: if we merely thought that happiness is good, error or mistake in thinking this would be logically possible, and this would be incompatible with the fact that happiness is something that we necessarily want.

My claim that the fact that one would enjoy doing something is necessarily a reason for doing it is of course compatible with its being a reason that may, in the circumstances, be outweighed or overridden by other considerations. The necessity here is in its being *a* reason, not necessarily a conclusive reason, i.e. in its bearing with some pressure on what it is a reason for; it is not to be confused with that necessity in which someone who has a (conclusive) reason for doing something *must* do that thing.

It follows from my account that if the question arises for *A* of whether to do *x*, and it is true that he would enjoy doing *x*, then he has a reason for doing *x* whether or not he wants to. It does not follow (to return to Hume's doctrine) that if he did *x* for that reason, i.e. because he would (he thought) enjoy doing it, a 'passion' would not be necessary to motivate his action. For if this is his reason for doing *x*, it follows that he thinks that he would enjoy doing it, and this implies that he in some way and to some degree wants to do it. The notion of somebody's wanting to do something is analytically connected with the notion of *his* reason, i.e. with his thinking that *p* is the case, not with the notion of there being a reason, i.e. with its actually being the case that *p*. One can question whether there is a reason for someone to do *x* by questioning, e.g. whether he would in fact enjoy doing *x*; but as long as this is his reason he certainly thinks that he would enjoy doing *x*, and there can then be no doubt that he wants to do it.

It also follows from my account that though such a fact as this, that one would enjoy doing something, is a reason for doing it, and can therefore, when somebody does something for that reason, explain why he did it, this fact is not a reason for wanting to do that thing and cannot explain in the same way why somebody wants to do it. It can, indeed, explain in some way why somebody wants to do something: for it rules out, e.g., the explanation that he wants to do it simply in order to do something else. I may want to go for a walk simply because I need the exercise, and it would be a different explanation to say that I want to go for a walk because I enjoy walking (and therefore would, I think, enjoy a walk on this occasion). But this explanation of my wanting to go for a walk is neither causal nor an explanation in terms of my reason for wanting to go for a walk; for thinking that one would enjoy doing something entails wanting to do it. The analogue to this in the theoretical field is the kind of case in which, as in 3.16, it is true not only that 'p' entails 'q' but also that 'A thinks that p' entails 'A thinks that q'. When this condition holds, the fact that p cannot be a reason for thinking that q; and in the practical case, similarly, the fact that one would enjoy doing x cannot be a reason for wanting to do it. We may therefore agree with Hume that in these cases at any rate a 'desire' is necessary if an action is to be performed, and also that such an ultimate desire has no rational justification in the sense that the fact that one would enjoy doing something is not a reason for wanting to do it. What does not follow is that this fact is not a reason for doing that thing.

Another thing that does not follow is that reasons of this sort, i.e. reasons such that, if they are the agent's reasons for doing something, imply that he wants to do that thing, are the only kind of reasons for doing things. This seems to me to be false. What is true, and perhaps sometimes confused with this falsehood, is that reasons of this sort are the most basic kind of practical reasons. There are, I think, other kinds of reasons for doing things, reasons of a sort such that their being some particular person's reasons for doing something does not imply that he wants to do that thing. Moral reasons seem to me to be of this kind. It may, of course, be the case that if someone's reasons for doing something are moral reasons he also, as a matter of fact, wants to do that thing, and perhaps wants to do it *because* he thinks he morally ought to do it; and it may be that someone who wants to do what he thinks he morally ought is in some sense a better person than one who does not. My point is only that the fact that something is someone's reason for doing or having done something does not itself imply, since it does not in the case of moral reasons imply, that that person wants or wanted to do that thing. Nevertheless, that there are reasons of this sort presupposes that considerations of the basic sort are also reasons for doing things. Basic reasons for doing things are basic in that sense: unless there were reasons connected in the way outlined with wanting to do things, and therefore with doing things, there could not be reasons of any other kind for doing things; and it is the empirical content of these basic reasons that provides, though far more indirectly than psychological hedonism supposes, and in many cases more indirectly than indirect utilitarianism supposes, the empirical content of reasons of any kind for doing things. Kant's notion of a holy will, i.e. of a being who could have reasons for doing things without wanting to do anything, is thus incoherent. On the other hand, the claim that these reasons are basic in this sense is to be distinguished, as it has not always been, from the erroneous view that in cases of conflict they are *overriding* reasons.

5.6. *Equally reasonable alternatives in conduct*

I turn now to an important difference between theoretical and practical reason, a difference that has in various ways, at least by implication, been noticed and remarked upon often enough before but almost always misinterpreted. Philosophers have sometimes tried to formulate a single basic principle or a set of principles determining what is rational in conduct, and the principles they have offered have been criticised on the ground that in some and perhaps most circumstances they do not uniquely determine a single action from the several alternative actions open to the agent. Kant's categorical imperative may be thought to fail in this way, and similar objections have been made to the intuitionist doctrine that there are several basic principles of conduct that are not reducible to or derivable from any single principle. Mill's general argument against this intuitionist position is instructive: '. . . whatever that standard is, there can be but one: for if there were several ultimate principles of conduct, the same conduct might be approved by one of those principles and condemned by another; and there would be needed some more general principle, as umpire between them'.[1] Given appropriate interpretations of 'the same conduct', 'approved', and 'condemned', it could of course be the case that if the same conduct, i.e. conduct of the same description, was approved by one principle and condemned by another these two principles would be inconsistent with each other. But this is not the mistake that Mill is attributing to his opponents: the remedy for such a mistake would be simply the rejection of one or both of the principles, not a more general principle to act as umpire between them. Mill is thinking of the possibility of a so-called 'conflict of duties' or 'conflict of obligations', a situation in which fulfilment of one obligation is incompatible with fulfilment of another, as when, e.g., one can keep a promise only by

[1] *System of Logic,* Book VI, ch. XII, § 7.

telling a lie. Does Mill's argument hold good in the light of such possibilities?

Why, we might ask, is it necessary for such a conflict to be resolved, and does the possibility of such conflict show the need, as Mill argues, for a more general principle that umpires between the two conflicting principles by indicating that, at least in the particular situation concerned, one of the obligations overrides or outweighs the other? It seems clear that the concept of reason itself allows this possibility, that alternative items, say x and y, should be *equally reasonable*. If the question is whether to do x or y, where x and y are incompatible actions, it may be that the reasons for and against doing x balance the reasons for and against doing y, so that, as we say, there is nothing to choose between doing x and doing y. Sometimes, of course, we might say this sort of thing as a confession of ignorance, implying that fuller knowledge of the relevant facts would show that one alternative was more reasonable than the other. But there is no logical necessity that this should be so. However full our knowledge of the relevant facts, it is analytically possible that doing x should be no more or less reasonable than doing y: and therefore that we can or may do either. The differing meanings of the words 'ought' and 'obligation' reflect this possibility. Like the word 'reason' the word 'obligation', but not the word 'ought', is a noun that can be qualified by words of comparative degree or strength, and obligations, like reasons, can conflict with, override, outweigh, or balance one another. The word 'ought', on the other hand, signifies the overall resultant pressure of reason, if any. Where x and y are incompatible actions, we may have an obligation to do x and an obligation to do y, as we may have reason to do x and reason to do y; but it cannot be the case that we ought to do x and that we ought to do y. What may be the case is that we ought to do x or y, where this does not mean that we ought to do x or ought to do y. When x and y are not only incompatible but also exhaust the analytic or empirical possibilities, e.g. when y is *not-x*, it will not of course be true that we *ought* to do x or y, though it will be true that we *must* do x or y, where the modal word expresses the pressure of theoretical not practical reason. When x and y do not exhaust the empirical (or, therefore, the analytic) possibilities but do exhaust the possibilities from the point of view of practical reason, it will again be true that we *must* do x or y, where it is the pressure of practical reason that the modal word expresses.

Here, then, we have uses of the word 'must' that express the need for doing either x or y, though it doesn't matter which we do. Does this need give rise to a need for 'some more general principle, as umpire between them'? When we must do x or y, and there is nothing to choose between them, we still need to choose between them; but not in accordance with some more general principle of the sort that Mill had in mind (even Mill's principle cannot rule out the logical possibility of there being equally reasonable but incompatible ways of promoting the greatest happiness of the greatest number). There is what in some sense is a rational method of choosing between the alternatives, though it does not appeal to reasons for or against either of those alternatives, since *ex hypothesi* the reasons for and against do not favour one rather than the other. When reason cannot decide, it may be reasonable to let chance decide, e.g. by tossing a coin, or drawing lots: i.e. by allowing some random factor to settle the issue arbitrarily. What makes this reasonable is that in cases in which different people's claims are in conflict it rules out, if fairly done, the possibility of personal bias in the choice made between the alternatives. Like justice chance also is blindfolded, and when a choice has to be made between equally reasonable alternatives, letting chance decide at least has the negative merit, in these circumstances, that reason has in any circumstances, of not allowing to some relevant considerations more weight than they actually have.

5.7. *Equally reasonable beliefs*

There seems to be no analogue of this situation for theoretical reason. It might be thought that this shows that from the point of view of reason practical matters are essentially more open, less decidable, than theoretical matters, that the role of reason in practice is limited in a way in which the role of reason in theory is not; and it might even be thought, contrary to what I have said in the preceding paragraph, that since reason may not uniquely determine what to do, the 'decision-gaps' have to be closed by emotion, feeling, passion, or some other 'subjective' factor. What we actually find if we compare practical and theoretical reason on this matter is a situation too complex to be summed up in any such simple fashion.

I have argued that the relation of reason to belief is shaped by the analytic connection between belief and truth, and in particular by the indistinguishability of the question whether it is right to think that p from the question whether p. Given that the question whether p has an answer, and is not to be rejected because it is unintelligible, or too vague, or presupposes things that are false, there are two logically possible answers, exhaustive and incompatible: 'p' (or 'It is true that p') and '$not\text{-}p$' (or 'It is false that p'). Any relevant considerations will speak for or against one or the other of these answers, and these considerations will therefore constitute reasons for accepting one or the other of these answers, i.e. for believing that p or for believing that $not\text{-}p$ (disbelieving that p). As I pointed out in 3.5, these two do not exhaust the possibilities with respect to believing things: there is the third possibility of not believing (or disbelieving) that p. However, reason's bearing on this third possibility is only a reflection of its bearing on the other two. We can, of course, sensibly say such things as 'There are reasons for not believing that p' and 'He had reason not to believe that p'. But to be intelligible such statements must be ways of saying things about reasons for believing or disbelieving that p. Usually, to say that there are reasons for not believing that p is to say that there are reasons for believing that $not\text{-}p$. When we say some such thing as 'He had reason not to believe that p' and do not mean that he had reason to believe that $not\text{-}p$ our meaning is that he had no reason to believe that p, or no more reason to believe that p than to believe that $not\text{-}p$: this is the kind of case in which, e.g., there is no evidence, or not enough evidence, one way or the other, or in which the evidence in favour is balanced by equally strong evidence against.

We have, then, this degree of similarity on this topic between theoretical and practical reason: incompatible beliefs can be equally reasonable. But though the concept of reason itself, permitting this general notion of equally reasonable alternatives, allows this possibility in respect of belief, the essential connection in the theoretical field between reason and truth differentiates it from its counterpart in the practical field. Though incompatible beliefs can be equally reasonable they cannot be equally true: one at least must be false, and that one it must be a mistake, and therefore wrong, to believe. When there is a divergence in this way between the appraisal that reason makes of beliefs and their presupposed basic mode of appraisal the former kind of appraisal is always subject to some qualification: in contrast to the situation in the practical field, the claim that two incompatible beliefs are equally reasonable necessarily imputes to the person who thinks so ignorance of some of the relevant considerations, sometimes made explicit by a rider such as 'in the circumstances', or 'in the light of the available evidence'; and the evaluative aspect of the appraisal that reason makes of a belief tends to be deflected by any divergence onto the person who holds that belief, the standard of reasonableness of belief being set, or at least influenced by, the standard of reasonableness of people, i.e. the standard of what, in the circumstances, and human limitations being what they are, a reasonable person could be expected to believe.

Does this difference between theoretical and practical reason show anything about the relative scope of reason in the two fields? It might seem to show, contrary to common philosophical conviction, that the uniquely decidable character of theoretical problems is due not to the superiority of reason in theoretical matters but to the presupposed mode of appraisal essentially connected with belief; and that conduct, having no such contrasting mode of appraisal, allows reason its full scope by allowing the notion of alternatives that are without qualification equally reasonable. Looked at in this way, the concept of reason may seem to be pulled out of shape by the concept of belief, or rather, it may seem as if its shape is maintained only by replacing a missing limb with an artificial one. On the other hand, however, it is not so much the concept of belief as the basic mode of appraising belief that is here putting the concept of reason under pressure. Belief itself is in fact better adapted than action to the fact that reason is a concept allowing the possibility of equally reasonable alternatives. In general, belief, like reason, and unlike action, can have degrees, and the degree of strength or weight of reason in favour of a belief can be matched by the intensity of that belief: an overwhelming or conclusive reason for thinking that p is a reason for being convinced that p, a strong reason is a reason for being fairly sure, and when the reasons against are somewhat weightier than those in favour one has reason to doubt whether p. In particular, if two incompatible beliefs are equally reasonable one can suspend judgment, and there is no necessity, as in the case of actions, for deciding between them, or for letting chance decide. It may be the case that one must believe the disjunction of the two: they may be exhaustive, i.e. 'p' and 'not-p', and one must believe that p or not-p; and if 'p' and 'q' are not exhaustive, but each is more reasonable than any third possibility, one must believe that p or q.

But one can believe that p or q without its being the case that one believes that p or believes that q. Since the notions of doing something and what one does are not related in the same way as the notions of believing something and what one believes, there is no such possibility in the case of action: to do x or y is to do x or do y. Action, we may say, unlike belief, is distributive through disjunction.

It might be objected that the distinction I am arguing for seems to hold only because I am misaligning the items, a misalignment that involves, among other things, an equivocation in the concept of incompatibility. For just as it is analytically necessary for anyone either to do x or not do x, so it is analytically necessary for anyone either to believe that p or not believe that p; and just as there can be no way of suspending action between the former alternatives, so there can be no way of suspending belief between the latter. Thus, when I suspend belief between two equally reasonable alternatives by believing that p or q, I am in fact, in rejecting both the belief that p and the belief that q, selecting the analytically necessary alternative of not believing that p and not believing that q.

The answer to this is contained in what I have already said about the distinctiveness of the relation of reason to belief, first adumbrated in 3.5. Anyone considering the question whether to believe that p or to believe that $not\text{-}p$ or not to believe (or disbelieve) that p is necessarily, by virtue of the transparency of belief, considering the question whether p; and any bearing that reason has on the answer to the former question will be a reflection of the bearing it has on the answer to the latter question. Now any consideration that has a bearing on the answer to this latter question will bear either in favour of or against the answer that p, i.e. will tend to show either that p or that $not\text{-}p$; and it will therefore, in its bearing on the answer to the former question, be a reason for or against believing that p, i.e. for believing that p or believing that $not\text{-}p$ (disbelieving that p). It is only if the reasons for and against are more or less balanced, including the special case in which there is no reason of sufficient weight for or against, that there can be reason neither to believe nor disbelieve that p. Thus in particular the alternative of not believing (or disbelieving) that p cannot be equally reasonable with, say, believing that p. For there are only three possible ways in which reason can bear on believing that p: there can be sufficient reason for, or against, believing that p, or no reason of sufficient weight either for or against. Not believing (or disbelieving) that p cannot be equally reasonable with believing that p in any of these cases. In the theoretical field, therefore, the notion of equal reasonableness is not only necessarily subject to qualification; it applies only, with respect to any proposition 'p', to believing and disbelieving that p, and never exhausts the possible 'propositional attitudes'. The complexity of the situation in the field of theoretical reason by comparison with the relative simplicity of the situation in the field of practical reason is a consequence of the fact that the essential normative connection between belief and truth, and therefore reason and truth, underlies this conceptual contrast, that there are only two truth-values (true and false) but many degrees of reason and belief.

5.8. *Imperative and indicative logic*

These arguments about the similarities and differences between belief and action and their respective relations to reason have been very general and abstract, but it is clear, as I have insisted, that ideas, and more generally misconceptions, about these matters are capable of determining views that are much more specific and detailed. I propose to conclude, therefore, by considering their relevance to a topic of apparently fine detail, but one which, as is commonly realised, raises problems of a general kind about the relations between practical reason and theoretical reason. I refer to the problem of the relations between indicative and imperative logic raised by the question whether the indicative entailment from 'p' to 'p or q' holds for imperatives. For this purpose I shall look at Hare's criticisms[1] of one of the central arguments in favour of the claim that imperatives and indicatives have fundamentally different logics. The argument Hare objects to is that the inference from 'p' to 'p or q' is valid if 'p' and 'q' are indicatives but invalid if they are imperatives: for if it is true that, e.g., Smith will post the letter, then it is true that Smith will post the letter or burn it; but from the imperative 'Post the letter' we cannot infer the imperative 'Post the letter or burn it', since this seems to give permission not to post the letter so long as one burns it. Part of Hare's objection is that this permission is not an entailment of the

[1] 'Some Alleged Differences Between Imperatives and Indicatives', *Mind*, vol. LXXVI, no. 303, July 1967.

disjunctive imperative, but (in the language of H. P. Grice)[1] a 'conversational implicature': i.e. the connection between the two is not a strictly logical connection mediated by rules of meaning but a connection resulting from certain general conventions of communication, such as that, unless there is good reason against doing so, one should commit oneself to a stronger rather than a weaker utterance if one is able to, e.g. to the statement that he posted the letter if one knows this, rather than to the disjunctive statement, also true but weaker, that either he posted it or he burned it. However, though according to Hare the imperative 'Post the letter or burn it' does not imply 'You may refrain from posting the letter so long as you burn it', he seems to agree that burning the letter and not posting it fulfils the disjunctive command. Thus, he claims, if I order someone to post the letter he may legitimately infer the weaker disjunctive command 'Post the letter or burn it', and though he may not from this infer the permission 'You may refrain from posting the letter so long as you burn it' he fulfils or obeys the disjunctive command if he burns the letter and does not post it. But then, says Hare, 'he has erred. But his error consists, not in making an invalid inference, but in fulfilling the weaker command when what I gave him was the stronger. We cannot in general be sure of fulfilling commands by fulfilling other commands which are inferable from them. We cannot, for example, fulfil the command "Put on your parachute and jump out" by just jumping out. In such cases the inferred command gives a necessary, but not a sufficient, condition for fulfilling the command from which it is inferred. In this respect commands are just like statements, except that fulfilment takes the place of belief (which is the form of acceptance appropriate to statements). If I am told "He has put on his parachute and jumped out", I am thereby licensed to accept or believe the statement which is inferable from it, "He has jumped out". But if I believe that that is all he has done, I am in error.'[2]

5.9. *The indicative analogy of action: belief or truth?*

It is clear that in considering the role of action in imperative logic analogies with indicative logic will pull us in two different directions. The relation of action to imperative, i.e. of fulfilling or

[1] In his paper in the Supplementary Volume of the *Proceedings of the Aristotelian Society,* 1961.
[2] op. cit., p. 313.

obeying an order, will on the one hand be construed on analogy with the way in which a situation or state of affairs fulfils or satisfies an indicative that describes it, and as the truth-conditions of an indicative determine its logical relations, so the obedience-conditions of an imperative will be regarded as determining its logical relations. On the other hand, the relation of action to imperative will be construed on analogy with the relation between a statement and acceptance of (i.e. belief in) that statement, so that acting on an imperative inferred from another imperative will be like inferring or drawing a conclusion from a premise. The way in which these analogies fall apart can be seen by considering what Hare offers[1] as 'a general rule, that two commands, or a command and a permission, are logically inconsistent if . . . it is logically impossible to act on both'. If we re-write this for indicatives in accordance with the above analogies, we get two versions, one of which gives a necessary and sufficient, the other only a sufficient, condition of inconsistency: the necessary and sufficient condition is that two statements are inconsistent if it is logically impossible for both to be fulfilled or satisfied, i.e. true; the merely sufficient condition is that two statements are inconsistent if it is logically impossible to accept both, i.e. to believe both. As I have argued, except in the special cases defined in 3.17, the bearing of truth-conditions on belief is normative, and it is in general inconsistent, but not logically impossible, to believe inconsistent things (3.14). Thus Hare's view that in the respect he mentions 'commands are just like statements, except that fulfilment takes the place of belief . . .' is unacceptable, and depends for its plausibility on an equivocation in the preceding sentence, namely 'the inferred command gives a necessary, but not a sufficient, condition for fulfilling the command from which it is inferred'. It is of course the case that the truth or fulfilment of a statement is a necessary but not a sufficient condition of the truth or fulfilment of any statement from which it can be inferred. But it is not in general the case that either the truth of or belief in a statement is a necessary condition of believing a statement from which it can be inferred. Pursuing his analogy, Hare says of indicative inference,[2] 'One cannot, in consistency, accept the premises without accepting the conclusion . . .'. But again the analogy fails, and in the same way: though it is inconsistent to accept the premise and reject the

[1] op. cit., p. 311.
[2] op. cit., p. 314.

conclusion of a valid inference, it is logically possible; whereas on Hare's view of imperative inference it would not be inconsistent but logically impossible to accept an imperative premise and reject any imperative validly inferrable from it, given that accepting an imperative is fulfilling (i.e. obeying) it. The fact is that, as Hare himself suggests in *The Language Of Morals*,[1] there are two different candidates for the notion of accepting an imperative: giving or agreeing with an order (etc.), and fulfilling (acting on) it. Given Hare's 'general rule', the former shares with acceptance of indicatives the logical possibility of accepting inconsistent things, but the latter does not; and in this respect the situation in which one person assents to another's indicative utterance is very unlike the situation in which one person assents to by acting on another's imperative utterance. On the other hand, since the acceptability of a transparent imperative is indistinguishable from the acceptability of the action it enjoins, there will be analogies between the way in which the logic of imperatives will bear on the acceptability of the actions they enjoin and the way in which the logic of indicatives bears on the acceptability of those indicatives.

Hare construes the idea that the imperative 'Post the letter or burn it' gives a necessary but not a sufficient condition of the command 'Post the letter' in such a way that it amounts to the true claim that the fulfilment of the latter necessarily fulfils the former: this of course is a claim in indicative logic that anyone who posts the letter either posts or burns it. As Hare points out, the converse does not necessarily hold: it is not necessarily the case that the fulfilment of the former fulfils the latter. He suggests that the sense in which the disjunctive utterance is a necessary but not sufficient condition of the non-disjunctive one is that the fulfilment of the former is a partial fulfilment, or fulfilment of a part, of the latter; and he illustrates this with the way in which a conjunctive utterance is partly fulfilled by fulfilment of one of the conjuncts ('He has put on his parachute and jumped out').

Those against whom Hare is arguing, however, may feel that this comparison is inept: it is not, they may say, that fulfilment of a disjunctive partly fulfils one of the disjuncts, for the state of affairs that fulfils a disjunctive is not even necessarily compatible with the state of affairs that fulfils one of the disjuncts. The fulfilment-conditions of 'p or q' are 'p and q', '$not\text{-}p$ and q', and 'p and $not\text{-}q$', and if the second condition holds the state of

[1] section 2.2.

affairs in virtue of which '*p* or *q*' is fulfilled, far from constituting a partial fulfilment of '*p*', will actually be incompatible with it. Does this distinguish the way in which '*p* or *q*' is a necessary condition of '*p*' from the way in which '*q*' is a necessary condition of '*p* and *q*'? The answer may seem to be in Hare's favour, that it does not. For the state of affairs that fulfils '*q*' is not necessarily compatible with the state of affairs that fulfils '*p* and *q*': with respect to '*p*' and '*q*' there are two fulfilment-conditions of '*q*', namely '*p* and *q*' and '*not-p* and *q*', and if the latter condition holds the state of affairs in virtue of which '*q*' is fulfilled will be incompatible with the fulfilment of '*p* and *q*'.

5.10. *Fulfilment-conditions, acceptance-conditions, and modality*

The principle that governs Hare's argument is a principle about fulfilment-conditions. His claim is in effect that whether they are indicatives or imperatives '*p*' entails '*q*' if the fulfilment of '*p*' necessarily fulfils '*q*'. However, the normative implications of entailment statements also require other conditions to be met, what we may call acceptance-conditions. Except for the kind of cases mentioned in 3.17, if '*p*' entails '*q*', '*q*' must be inferable from '*p*', i.e. acceptance of '*p*' must commit one to acceptance of '*q*', and more weakly acceptance of '*q*' must be (at least) consistent with acceptance of '*p*'. Hare's example of inferring one conjunct from a conjunction meets this weak condition. Believing that he has jumped out is consistent with believing that he has put on his parachute and jumped out. The error that Hare alludes to is the error of believing that he has jumped out and that is all he has done, i.e. that he has not put on his parachute. But anyone who inferred this from the statement 'He has put on his parachute and jumped out' would be making an invalid inference, contrary to Hare's description of the error in what he takes to be the analogous imperative case: he is not licensed to infer any such thing, because accepting it would be inconsistent with accepting what it is inferred from. This weak condition, that accepting what is entailed by an utterance must be consistent with accepting what entails it, is also met for the indicative entailment from '*p*' to '*p* or *q*'. But is it met for the imperative case? If accepting an imperative is acting in accordance with it, then acceptance here, in contrast to the indicative case, is identical with fulfilment. We have seen that the fulfilment of '*p*' necessarily fulfils '*p* or *q*'; but we have also seen that the fulfilment of '*p* or *q*' is not necessarily compatible with the fulfilment of '*p*', i.e. when '*p* or *q*' is fulfilled by '*not-p* and *q*'. Thus acceptance of 'Post the letter or burn it' by burning the letter and not posting it is incompatible with acceptance of 'Post the letter'; whereas it is not true, as Hare suggests, that acceptance of 'He has jumped out' is incompatible with acceptance of 'He has put on his parachute and jumped out'. Accepting 'He has jumped out' is accepting part of 'He has put on his parachute and jumped out': but accepting 'Post the letter or burn it' by burning it and not posting it cannot be accepting part of something it is inconsistent with, namely 'Post the letter'.

Does this not raise a problem about the indicative entailment from '*p*' to '*p* or *q*'? How is it possible, it might be asked, that acceptance of '*p* or *q*' is necessarily compatible with acceptance of '*p*' when the state of affairs that fulfils '*p* or *q*' is not necessarily compatible with the state of affairs that fulfils '*p*'? And similarly, in Hare's conjunctive example, how is it possible that accepting '*q*' is necessarily compatible with accepting '*p* and *q*', though '*q*' is fulfilled by '*not-p* and *q*', which is incompatible with the fulfilment of '*p* and *q*'? The answer is the same in both cases. Fulfilment is distributive through disjunction: the fulfilment of '*p* or *q*' is the fulfilment of '*p* and *q*' or the fulfilment of '*not-p* and *q*' or the fulfilment of '*p* and *not-q*'. Where acceptance is not identical with fulfilment, e.g. where what is accepted are indicatives and the mode of acceptance is belief, acceptance (though distributive through conjunction) is not distributive through disjunction: a disjunctive belief is not a disjunction of beliefs, so that believing that *p* or *q* is believing that *p* and *q* or *not-p* and *q* or *p* and *not-q*; it is not believing that *p* and *q* or believing that *not-p* and *q* or believing that *p* and *not-q*. Since acceptance of '*p* or *q*' does not commit me to acceptance of '*not-p* and *q*', and since in the indicative case it is logically possible for me to accept '*p* or *q*' without accepting any one of the disjuncts that constitute the fulfilment-conditions of '*p* or *q*', accepting the indicative '*p* or *q*' neither commits me to accepting nor licenses me to accept the indicative '*not-p* and *q*'. In the imperative case, where acceptance is fulfilment, acceptance is distributive through disjunction, and if I accept '*p* or *q*' it is logically necessary for me either to accept '*p* and *q*' or to accept '*not-p* and *q*' or to accept '*p* and *not-q*'. Consequently, since '*p* or *q*' does not say which, accepting it does not commit me to accepting, but it must license me to accept, '*not-p* and *q*'. In Hare's conjunctive case, believing that *q* commits me to believing that q and p or *not-p* but it does not commit me to believing either of the disjuncts, nor does it permit me to believe either. 'p or *not-p*' is the tautology of fulfilment-conditions, i.e. it exhausts the fulfilment possibilities (and therefore the possibilities of action). But it does not represent the tautology of acceptance-conditions, either for belief or from the point of view of the person giving an imperative.

Given that the notion of an imperative is related in the foregoing way to that of accepting an imperative, with accepting an imperative identified with acting on it, so that acceptance-conditions are fulfilment-conditions and therefore analogous to truth-conditions in indicative logic, this notion will determine a correlative notion of giving or agreeing with an imperative, e.g. a command, and therefore, if you wish, another mode or sense of accepting an imperative. This notion of accepting an imperative will bear to the other notion relations analogous in some respects to those which the notion of accepting an indicative (belief) bears to fulfilment (truth). In particular, like belief and unlike fulfilment, it will not be distributive through disjunction: a disjunctive command will be distinguishable from a disjunction of commands. Of course, the same form of words might be used for both: to give an example from Hare to which this point is relevant, 'Go *via* Coldstream or Berwick'. If this is a disjunctive command, acceptance of it by the person to whom it is addressed will involve his fulfilling it, i.e. satisfying one of its set of fulfilment-conditions; and his acceptance of it, therefore, will require him to interpret it as licensing him not to fulfil one of the disjuncts as long as he fulfils the other, i.e. to interpret it as 'Go *via* Coldstream or Berwick, it doesn't matter which'. If it is interpreted in the way Hare suggests, from the point of view of the person giving the command, as 'Go *via* Coldstream or Berwick, I'm not yet saying which' or 'Go *via* Coldstream or Berwick, I don't yet know which', acceptance of it by the person to whom it is addressed cannot be identical with his fulfilling it; for it is not a disjunctive command but a disjunction of commands, i.e. it is not a single command but two commands. That is, the speaker's utterance does not have a set of fulfilment-conditions; rather, each disjunct has its own set of fulfilment-conditions. If choice between the two commands is to be settled by further information, as in Hare's example, a single command can be given (and accepted, i.e. acted on, by the person to whom it is addressed): this will be a conjunction of hypothetical imperatives (though not in Kant's sense), e.g. 'If the Coldstream route is open go *via* Coldstream, and if it is not go *via* Berwick'. In arguing that his example 'shows that "Do *a* or do *b*" does not entail "You may do *a*" but only conversationally implicates it',[1] Hare is thus correct if by this he means that the ordinary use of the word 'or' allows a construction in which 'Do *a* or do *b*' is a disjunction of commands not a disjunctive command. But to the extent that his imperative logic allows disjunction to function in that way, to that extent it will defeat any aim he may have of developing an imperative logic that is isomorphous with the indicative logic of the propositional calculus.

The fundamental point of conflict in Hare's views on this subject is between the following two ideas: that a logic of imperatives can be constructed which is isomorphous with the indicative logic of the propositional calculus, and which, like that logic, is non-modal; and that, in accordance with his prescriptivism, accepting an imperative is fulfilling it. Much of my argument through this book has sought to establish that logical relations between items have a modal, and in general normative, bearing on accepting those items. If that is so, and if accepting an imperative if fulfilling it, the basic notion of fulfilment-conditions, essential to the propositional calculus, must in an imperative logic have a modal interpretation.

---

[1] op. cit., p. 316.

INDEX